The politics
of the school curriculum

Denis Lawton

Routledge & Kegan Paul
London, Boston and Henley

First published in 1980
by Routledge & Kegan Paul Ltd
39 Store Street, London WC1E 7DD,
9 Park Street, Boston, Mass. 02108, USA and
Broadway House, Newtown Road,
Henley-on-Thames, Oxon RG9 1EN
Set in 11/12 IBM Press Roman by Columns
and printed in Great Britain by
Lowe & Brydone Printers Ltd.
Thetford, Norfolk

British Library Cataloguing in Publication Date

Lawton, Denis
The politics of the school curriculum. – (Routledge
education books).
1. Education and state – Great Britain.
2. Education – Great Britain – Curricula
I. Title
375'.00941   LC93.G7   79 41694
ISBN 0 7100 0567 9
ISBN 0 7100 0568 7 Pbk

The politics
of the school curriculum

Routledge Education Books

Advisory editor: John Eggleston
Professor of Education
University of Keele

Contents

Preface

For a number of years my colleagues and I at the London Institute of Education Curriculum Studies Department have been using an approach to curriculum studies which has as its central concept the definition of curriculum in terms of 'a selection from the culture of a society'. This has proved very fruitful, but occasionally the obvious question is asked: 'Who selects?'. Our general answer has been a simple one — 'teachers'. This is a useful answer because part of our purpose has been to encourage all teachers to be more aware both of the necessity to think clearly about their contribution to the curriculum and also about the need for planning the whole curriculum.

But the answer that teachers make the selection from the culture is only true in a limited way. We have also to analyse the various constraints on teachers' freedom: the DES, inspectors, LEAs, examinations and so on. What kind of influence or control is exerted by all these? At the present time this is an even more important question because the picture is a changing one — for example, there are faint but discernible signs that the DES is attempting to exert more central influence.

The picture is not a clear one, but it seemed an appropriate time to attempt to sketch out various influences on the curriculum. The sketch is tentative and incomplete: there are serious gaps in the general picture. For example, we know far too little about the functioning of LEAs in relation to school curricula (Kogan's excellent book about the role of the Chief Education Officer, *County Hall* (1973), does not have a single entry for curriculum in the index). Much basic research work remains to be done in this field, but it was felt that enough important changes were being discussed – the Schools Council, the APU, examinations – to justify the publication of a deliberately polemical book about curriculum control.

I would like to thank those colleagues and students (MA, 1979) who made helpful comments on an earlier draft.

Acknowledgments

The author and publishers would like to thank the following: the Department of Education and Science for permission to quote from *Educating our Children: Four Subjects for Debate* (1977), *Education in Schools: a Consultative Document* (1977) and Circular 14/77; the editor of *Trends in Education* for permission to quote from 'Monitoring Pupil's Performance' by B. W. Kay which appeared in *Trends in Education*, 1975/2; the editor of the *Cambridge Journal of Education* for permission to quote from 'Rethinking Case Study: Notes from the Second Cambridge Conference', by C. Adelman, D. Jenkins and S. Kemmis, which appeared in vol. 6, no. 3, 1976.

Chapter 1

The meaning of politics

This book is not mainly about party politics and the curriculum, but about the question 'who controls the curriculum of secondary schools?' The answer is not a simple one, and the question itself is of fairly recent origin, only becoming important when the curriculum began to be called into question. When there was no controversy about the content of the curriculum, there was no argument about its control. When the curriculum becomes controversial, however, it is essentially a political controversy. There are two interrelated problems: the distribution of knowledge in society; and the decision-making involved.

If we take 1944 as a crucial date in the development of secondary education, it would be true to say that the following ten years or so were dominated by the debate about the tripartite system: should there be separate schools for different kinds of ability or comprehensive schools catering for all children? By the late 1950s that battle was largely over, and for about the next ten years the discussion shifted to questions of grouping and school organisation: should comprehensive schools be divided vertically into houses or horizontally into year groups? Should we have streaming, or setting, or banding, or mixed ability groups?[1] By 1965 these questions about structure had developed, to some extent, into questions about the content of the curriculum, partly stimulated by the work of the Schools Council.[2] At the same time some educationists began asking the more fundamental question 'What is the point of a common school unless we have a

1

common curriculum which transmits a common culture?'

By the mid-1960s it was also becoming clear that the period of consensus in education since 1944 had obscured a number of fundamental ideological problems about the nature of education. From then on disputes often centred on the question of 'the comprehensive school' but they went much deeper than a difference of opinion about whether grammar schools should survive or not. The Black Papers[3] (from 1969 onwards) helped to illustrate at least two of these areas of conflict: whether schools should concentrate on an elite few or on the majority; whether the purpose of education was to develop individuals or to socialise children to fit in to the existing social structure.

On the first of those issues the Labour Party has always been divided, and that is one reason for deciding to avoid identifying party politics with the politics of the curriculum: it is much more complicated than a simple left *versus* right confrontation. Within the Labour Party, many individuals valued grammar schools because they had helped bright working-class youngsters to climb the ladder of opportunity: for this group of politicians (and many others) comprehensive schools would only be 'successful' if they enabled more working-class pupils to climb even higher up the ladder and away from their own social origins. For such Labour Party 'elitists' an important feature of comprehensive schools would be selection and streaming so that the 'able' would be helped on their journey upwards and not held back by those less gifted.

This debate goes back a long way in labour history. As early as 1897 the Trades Union Congress had demanded a policy of secondary education for all, condemning the segregation of elementary and secondary-school pupils. At that stage they were firmly against the elitist basis of the grammar-school curriculum. But the Fabian Society, and in particular Sidney and Beatrice Webb, had pursued a policy very much in the liberal tradition of utilitarian philosophy, justifying selection on grounds of economic and social efficiency.[4] So there is a fundamental difference in outlook, even between those in the same political party (the Labour Party); it may be convenient to label one group egalitarians and the other elitists, although this terminology is not entirely satisfactory. Egalitarians want a worthwhile curriculum for all children; elitists are concerned to select the brightest for a superior, academic curriculum.

The question 'who shall be educated?' is clearly related to the question of 'what are schools for?' – is it to make life more worthwhile for all individuals, or to make society work more efficiently? Sidney and Beatrice Webb and many early Fabians belonged to the philosophical tradition which emphasised education as a means of making society a better place in the sense of a more efficient organisation. Sidney Webb's book *London Education* (1904) described the kind of 'capacity catching' machinery of scholarships which would ensure efficient leadership for society at home and in the British Empire. Webb was totally opposed to the idea of a common school with a common curriculum, and accepted the Morant policy (1902-4) of sharp differentiation between elementary and secondary curricula. In fact Sidney Webb's views were so similar to the Conservative policy on secondary education at that time that in January 1901 Sir John Gorst, the Conservative education minister, distributed proof copies of Webb's Fabian Manifesto *The Educational Muddle and the Way Out* in support of the Conservative policy of clearly separating elementary and secondary schools, but providing a scholarship ladder which would enable a few very bright working-class children to pass from elementary schools into the secondary schools.[5] In the House of Commons the two members sponsored by the Labour Representative Committee (the precursor of the Parliamentary Labour Party) opposed the 1902 Education Bill; at that time the majority of the Labour Movement was on their side, but an influential part of the Fabian Society had firmly established a non-socialist tradition which the Labour Party was later to inherit and to preserve.

The Labour Movement as a whole tended to see the 1902 Act as a piece of class legislation. In their social and educational views the Labour Movement covered a very wide range: 'Elitism and egalitarianism with Webb at one end, Thorne and Hobson at the other, and the ILP somewhere in the middle, provided the limits within which Labourism was

3

set rather than the framework on which it was built' (Barker, 1972, p. 18).[6] The dispute was, of course, not simply about the structure of education into secondary and elementary: the content of the curriculum was at stake as well.

A more recent version of the dispute between egalitarians and elitists centres on the word 'meritocratic'. In 1958 Michael Young published *The Rise of the Meritocracy*, which should have succeeded in demolishing the meritocratic point of view. The book was described as a fable narrating the development of a meritocratic society some time in the future. A society (England in the future) is described where 'I.Q. plus effort = merit'.[7] This was a society where the most intelligent had to be detected at an early age and given the opportunity to benefit from an intensive educational programme. If they responded with appropriate effort they were ultimately rewarded by being allotted a position in life in accordance with their carefully calculated 'merit'. It was, needless to say, described as a nightmare world where efficiency took precedence over humanity, and where those who lacked measured ability were destined to a carefully planned inferior life. Implicitly the question was asked (which had been ignored by many who considered themselves to be concerned with social justice): if it is unfair for children to have a better education because they happen to be born rich, is it any less unfair for children to have preferential treatment because they happen to be born with a high IQ?

One of the messages in Young's book was that the meritocratic position rests on an inadequate view of democracy: true democracy in a free society should include a better quality of life for *all*, and the vast majority of the population should have access to worthwhile educational experiences, not just an elite few — whether they are a social or an intellectual elite.

So one 'political' dispute about the curriculum is whether an educational programme should be planned for the most able pupils which is quite different in content and form from the curriculum designed for the majority. A related (but distinct) question is whether there should be a curriculum planned for all pupils which has some common elements.

If it is decided to give a superior curriculum to the elite

4

and an inferior curriculum to the majority, then two kinds of decisions must be made. First, it is necessary to decide who goes into which category; second, it is necessary to decide what kind of curriculum would be suitable for those two groups. Both decisions are essentially political: the first decision exerts control over who is to have access to the power bestowed by certain kinds of knowledge; the second involves a judgment about the relative statuses of kinds of knowledge – a judgment which, of course, tends to confirm those statuses.

If a preference is expressed for concentrating on providing a common curriculum, then the first decision (that is allocation to two different levels of curricula) is avoided, but not the second – the determination of what will go into a common curriculum. But perhaps the second question is not as difficult as it seems. The argument in favour of a common curriculum is usually made along one or more of the following three lines:

1   Comprehensive schools were introduced partly to equalise opportunities, that is, to give groups such as working-class children and girls of all classes a better education. But if you divide children into categories at an early stage of their education (academic and non-academic; grammar and modern) and give them different curricula, then you effectively prevent those following a non-academic curriculum ever becoming 'academic': they cannot 'catch up' because they are effectively running in a separate race. The benefits of comprehensive schools can be nullified by curricular differentiation at too early a stage.

2   A second argument in favour of comprehensive schools was that separate schools tended to divide pupils socially and culturally as well as intellectually. Common schools help to 'unify society'; but this social and cultural unification would only take place if there were some kind of genuine common experience – a common curriculum – within the common schools. Otherwise, as Julienne Ford pointed out (1969), the divided system was simply perpetuated under one roof by means of 'streams' which possessed quite different 'cultures'. It might be argued that television has done more

for cultural unification than education, but that does not negate the argument that schools have a part to play in unifying society.

3   A third argument for a common curriculum is not necessarily connected with comprehensive schools at all. It suggests that if the state makes education compulsory for the 5-16 age group, then (because we value freedom highly in our society) it is the duty of the state to specify as far as possible the advantages to be gained by the child to compensate for eleven years' loss of freedom. At first these advantages tended to be taken for granted — it was simply assumed that education was 'a good thing'; but when education as an institution comes under attack then that assumption can no longer be taken for granted, and has to be justified in rational terms. Such a justification is difficult, if not impossible, without an explicit statement about the benefits bestowed by education in terms of curriculum content. This should be based upon a cultural analysis of the knowledge and skills which young people need in our society and the kinds of experiences that can be regarded as sufficiently 'worthwhile' to be made available for all.

If it is argued that education is not mainly about making society efficient, but is more concerned with giving as many people as possible access to a worthwhile life, then the problem of curriculum planning is not seen as the need to supply trained manpower for industry but as making a selection of the most important aspects of culture for transmission to the next generation. Then the crucial cultural question is 'what is worthwhile?', and the crucial political question is 'who makes the selection?'

Some recent sociologists specialising in the sociology of knowledge would have us believe that control of the curriculum is simply a question of bourgeois hegemony.[8] They assume that in a capitalist society the whole of the cultural superstructure, including education, is a reflection of the values of the dominant group — i.e. the bourgeoisie or the capitalist ruling class. For this group of writers education is assumed to be a totally socialising influence. But I am suggesting that the question of the control of education and the content of education is much more complicated than that — especially in a pluralist society. As I have argued that point in detail elsewhere (Lawton, 1975), in this book I would prefer to concentrate on the task of analysing who makes the decisions in our society about the organisation, the content and the planning of the curriculum. As well as questions about 'who?', there are related questions about 'how?' and 'why?'

One familiar answer to the question of 'who controls the curriculum?' is that in the UK, unlike any other country, teachers decide on their own curriculum — teachers are free to make their own selection. Teachers in England and Wales are certainly more free in this respect than in most other systems, but it would be a mistake to over-simplify the situation by exaggerating teachers' autonomy (as we shall see in Chapter 2). Secondary teachers' freedom to select their own curriculum content has legally existed only since 1945, and is today increasingly under attack.

Another familiar view is that in England and Wales we have a national system of education which is locally administered, leaving the implementation in the hands of teachers themselves. This may be seen in terms of a triangle of power: the central authority (DES), the local authority (LEAs) and the teachers.

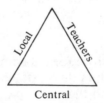

Figure 1.1

As we shall see in Chapter 2, there is an important ambiguity in this 'triangle'. 'The teachers' can refer either to the organised bodies of teachers (teachers' unions and professional associations) or to the fact that whatever the central or local authority may prescribe, the interpretation of the curriculum must always be in the hands of teachers.[9] If power is measured in terms of the length of each side of the triangle, it is clearly possible to have triangles of different shapes: in other words it would be a mistake to assume either that the triangle is equilateral or that angles do not change from time to time, especially if we are concerned with the control of the curriculum.

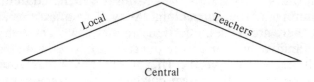

Central

Figure 1.2 Nineteenth century?

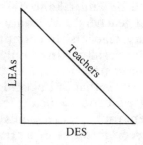

DES

Figure 1.3 Post-1945?

It may be useful to begin with a description of the formal position of each of these three 'partners' in relation to the secondary curriculum:

1   *The DES* now has little formal control over the curriculum. The word curriculum does not appear in the 1944 Education Act (which is still the major piece of legislation governing education); and no curriculum content is legally specified in secondary schools apart from religious instruction. But that does not necessarily mean that there could be no central influence or even control under the 1944 Act. As we shall see later, the 1977 Green Paper on Education makes great play with the notion that the Secretary of State cannot abdicate from curricular responsibilities; and this may be a hint of a swing back to central influence. It might be argued that the general description in the 1944 Act of the relation between local education authorities and the Secretary of

State should also apply to the school curriculum: it is stated that it is the Secretary of State's responsibility to 'secure the effective execution by local authorities, under his control and direction, of the national policy . . .'. It should also be added that the DES has powerful allies in the form of HMIs ('the eyes and ears of the Secretary of State'). If there were a central policy on the secondary curriculum (either public or secret) then HMIs could certainly be concerned with its enforcement.

But is there such a central policy? Up to 1944 there certainly was. Until they were swept away by the Education Act there was a powerful set of regulations which HMIs and LEAs used as one yardstick when looking at secondary schools. Since 1944-5 until the 1970s there seemed to be no central policy on curriculum. But are there signs of a resurgence of interest in control at the centre? Or at least a desire for more power than has existed in recent years? The Green Paper of 1977 combined with the HMI document *Curriculum 11-16* would seem to suggest so. But more of that in later chapters.

2   *Local Education Authorities* interpret the legislation and Circulars from central government; they also decide what schools to build, and how to organise them; LEAs, not central government, appoint and pay the teachers, supply books and equipment to the schools. The exact relationship between the DES and LEAs is not always clear, nor is the distribution of power between them, as can be seen from the Tameside dispute in 1977. This dispute concerned the decision of the LEA not to introduce the remaining stages of a comprehensive scheme which had been initiated by Tameside under Labour control. In May 1976 control passed to the Conservatives, who decided to stop the scheme, retain grammar schools and 11-plus selection. The Secretary of State issued a direction to Tameside to carry out the previous scheme, but the LEA appealed and the Court of Appeal maintained that the Secretary of State had inadequate grounds for concluding that the proposed action of Tameside was unreasonable. The House of Lords upheld this decision which could only be reversed by Parliamentary legislation.

The control of the curriculum has, however, not yet been a

subject which has caused conflict between the DES and LEAs. LEAs, although technically responsible for the curriculum of schools, have traditionally (that is, since 1945) left the control of the curriculum to governers who have normally left it to the head teachers, who may or may not leave it to their assistants.[10]

But once again the situation may be changing. In recent years LEAs have been criticised for neglecting the control of the curriculum or for having inadequate means of control (for example, the Auld Report was severely critical of the ILEA); and part of the follow-up to the Great Debate and the DES Green Paper of 1977 was an LEA curriculum survey (Circular 14 of 1977).[11] The 1976-8 constitutional review of the Schools Council also involved some criticism of LEAs for failing to take sufficient initiative in curriculum planning and development. (A seriously neglected area of research is the analysis of the part played by LEA Advisors and Inspectors in the control and development of curriculum.)

3   *The teachers*, in *any* system, effectively have a good deal of control over the curriculum, in the sense of what actually gets taught and how it gets taught. Even if some curriculum content is centrally prescribed, control over the way it is transmitted leaves a good deal of power in the hands of the teachers. (How important that is in terms of influencing the minds of the young is another matter! There is probably a tendency to exaggerate the power of the teacher in this respect.) In England and Wales teachers have, in addition to this control of the manner of transmission, more power to decide on what should be transmitted than almost any other group of teachers. As we shall see in Chapter 2, the extent of teachers' power as curriculum decision-makers is frequently exaggerated, but despite the constraints imposed by examinations, HMIs, LEA Inspectors, governors and head teachers, it remains true to say that teachers have a high degree of professional autonomy, which they fought for in the nineteen century and gained after 1944. In addition, teachers' unions and professional associations are formally recognised and extremely influential politically (see Manzer, 1970). They have made teachers' professional autonomy a central plank of their policy.

In recent years, however, this autonomy has been questioned and challenged by a number of groups and for a variety of different reasons, many of them connected with 'accountability'.

Accountability

Accountability has become a much used (and misused) term in education in recent years. Essentially accountability is concerned with the idea that those entrusted with money or responsibility for doing something should 'give an account' of what they have done (including how they have spent the money). Government ministers, for example, are accountable in a general sense to Parliament, and the doctrine of ministerial responsibility may require them to resign for decisions made by their subordinates; they are also accountable in a particular financial sense through the Public Accounts Committee serviced by the Comptroller and Auditor General. All such accountability is political in the sense that one level in a hierarchical system is subject to scrutiny by a different level. It may be worth observing at this stage that democratic accountability is not simply a subordinate being accountable to his superiors but also someone at the top of a hierarchy (e.g. a minister) being accountable to those of a technically lower status.

Accountability as such is no new phenomenon, but it has taken a new turn in education in recent years. It has increasingly been suggested that teachers should be more accountable to the public. As we shall see, this has given rise to demands for more parents to be included on governing bodies, and for these bodies to have more power and control over the curriculum (see the Taylor Report, 1977 and the Education Act 1978).[12]

One reason for the demand for greater accountability in education in the 1970s was the economic climate. When funds are in short supply there is a tendency for politicians and rate-payers to demand 'value for money'. This financial motive in the 1970s coincided with at least two other powerful factors: the first was a general move toward greater parti-

11

cipation by the public in administrative affairs (especially in this case by parents); the second was a general disillusionment with education — a movement which started in the 1960s, reached a Conservative climax with the first Black Paper in 1969 and a Labour climax in the Prime Minister's Ruskin speech in October 1976. All this was helped by such incidents as the William Tyndale School affair. That aspect of accountability will be considered in Chapter 2; an equally important aspect of accountability — the secrecy stance (and therefore lack of accountability) maintained by the DES — will be explored as part of Chapter 3.

It is important to stress that accountability should be regarded as a neutral term: accountability is neither good nor bad in itself. Certain kinds of accountability in education are highly desirable in an open society, but some kinds of accountability (e.g. some US styles of evaluation) are ill-conceived, mischievous and harmful to education. This will also be explored in later chapters.

The control of the curriculum is thus a very complex issue. It is of particular interest now for two reasons: more people want to know the answer; but the 'answer' itself is subject to change. We are witnessing a quiet struggle for control and influence. One interesting feature of the struggle and the changing scene is the shift in the dominant metaphor: from 'partnership' to 'accountability'. 'Partnership' indicates satisfaction and trust; 'accountability', dissatisfaction and distrust.

Summary

1   The politics of the curriculum is concerned with the distribution and control of worthwhile and relevant educational knowledge and experience.

2   This leads to two fundamental questions: what is a worthwhile curriculum? And who decides?

3   The conventional answer in terms of a simple pattern of partnership (between DES, LEAs and teachers) is yielding to a much more complex pattern of accountability.

4   The rest of this book is mainly concerned with some aspects of the changing pattern of curricular decision-making, and the decision-makers.

Chapter 2

Teachers and the control of the curriculum

One of the myths about secondary education in England is that there is a long tradition of teacher control over the curriculum. Bell and Grant (1974) have however pointed out that even in Elizabethan times the curriculum of grammar schools had been subject to close government scrutiny and interference. More recently there was strict control of the secondary curriculum from 1902 until secondary regulations were superseded by the 1944 Education Act. Elementary-school teachers, in the nineteenth century fought against rigid central control of the curriculum and succeeded in the twentieth century in shaking off this control almost completely. In recent years, however, there has been a certain loss of power by teachers for a variety of reasons which will be explored in this chapter and in later chapters.

The nineteenth-century background

Until 1833 there was little problem about state control of the curriculum because the government had deliberately avoided financial involvement and had left control of elementary schools to religious bodies. Attempts by Brougham in 1816 and 1818 to involve the government in elementary education had failed, largely because his proposals were extremely ambitious, involving too much expense and too much government interference.[1] A conflict was developing between those who in general held the philosophy of *laissez-faire* and those

13

who wanted some kinds of limited government intervention. In the field of education some retained a fear of government domination, but others believed that an exception to non-intervention should be made in the case of education, for both religious and political reasons. The 'lower orders' were feared because they were ungodly non-readers of the Bible, as well as dangerously undisciplined and ignorant electors after 1867.

In 1833 the radical MP John Roebuck asked the House of Commons to consider 'the means of establishing a system of national education' on the grounds that it would promote political tranquillity and public virtue. It is perhaps worth noting the political origins of our supposedly non-political education system. This scheme was also too ambitious and was unacceptable partly because it involved state control of teaching methods and curriculum. Although the Commons might have gone some way in the direction of relaxing the doctrine of *laissez-faire* in the specific case of education, they were unwilling to give so much power and control to the state (which was still regarded as a necessary evil rather than a means of generating good). There was, however, considerable support for the idea of giving some financial help towards the education of the poor; eighteen days later Lord Althorp, Chancellor of the Exchequer, discreetly included in the Report of the Committee of Supply a sum of up to £20,000 for education. This method of allocating money to education had the additional advantage of not being open to amendment by the House of Lords. The £20,000 was made available to the two religious societies for the purpose of building new schools, to make up deficiencies in areas where schools were particularly lacking. It has been pointed out that this was, even in those days, a very modest sum of money to spend on education, less in fact than was voted for renovating the royal stables in the same year.

For ideological reasons the government of the day preferred to hand over the control of the spending of the money and the control of the curriculum to religious societies rather than have any kind of government control. However, six years later, in 1839, the amount of money needed had increased dramatically, and was continuing to increase; a

14

Committee of the Privy Council was accordingly set up to supervise the spending of the money being annually granted by Parliament. The Council had a permanent staff – Dr Kay (later Sir James Kay-Shuttleworth[2]) as Secretary, and the Reverend Mr Allen and Mr Tremenheere as the first HM Inspectors of schools. Kay made the award of grants conditional upon favourable reports by his two HMIs.

Much excitement and suspicion was generated by this allocation of state funds to assist elementary education, and even more by the appointment of state officials to supervise the expenditure. There was a famous speech by Macaulay in the education debate of 1847 which boldly asked whether it was in fact inconsistent with civil and religious freedom that the state should take charge of the education of the people. He had to argue his case very convincingly because many who were 'nonconformists' in religion thought that it was extremely dangerous for something as important as education to get into the hands of a state where the official religion was the still very powerful Church of England; the Established Church was equally worried that it would lose some of its religious authority in the control of education to the growing state apparatus.

Despite the innovation of state supervision, the amount of money spent on education continued to grow. In 1858 a Commission was appointed under the chairmanship of the Duke of Newcastle 'to enquire into the present state of popular education in England, and to consider and report what measures, if any, are required for the extension of sound and cheap elementary instruction to all classes of the people'. This was an extensive review of popular education; and one of the findings was that teachers tended to neglect the more elementary subjects. The Commissioners were also particularly concerned that only about half of the pupils in elementary schools were being inspected by HMIs. The Commissioners felt

that there is only one way of securing this result, which is to institute a searching examination by a competent authority of every child in every school to which grants are to be paid with the view of ascertaining whether these

15

indispensable elements of knowledge are thoroughly acquired and to make the prospects and position of the teacher dependent, to a considerable extent, on the results of this examination. (Newcastle Report, vol. 1, p. 157)

So the idea of using tests as a means of judging not only pupil performance but also teacher efficiency has a long history in this country. 'Payment by results' was to become one of the major disputes between teachers and central authority throughout the nineteenth century, and lives on into the folk memory of teachers well into the twentieth century. The suggestion of 'payment by results' made by the Newcastle Commission became part of the 1862 Revised Code which set out the conditions on which grants were to be paid.[3] The Code stated specifically the content of the elementary school curriculum in terms of the three Rs (together with plain needlework for girls). So the early state control of the elementary curriculum might be said to be not only political but sexist! The pupils were examined in six stages or standards, the first to be taken by children of six years of age. Grants were to be paid to schools, no longer on the basis of the qualifications of the teachers, but on the results of an annual examination of all children in the school on the narrowly prescribed curriculum.

Payment by results, although considerably modified in the following years by successive Codes, lasted in some form until nearly the end of the century. The motive for this kind of central control was complex: on the one hand the middle classes wanted constant reassurances that they were getting value for the money spent on elementary education; on the other hand they were concerned that the education provided for the lower orders should not be so good that it would present a threat to the education of their own children, for which they paid fees. Both of these reasons could be regarded as political as could the third: the 1862 Code can also be seen as an early attempt to keep teachers in their correct place in society. Robert Lowe stated that: 'Teachers desiring to criticise the Code were as impertinent as chickens wishing to decide the sauce in which they would be served.'[4]

The growth of central control

The expansion of education after the 1870 Act (which laid the foundation for universal elementary education) would probably have diminished the ability of HMIs to control the curriculum in any case, unless their numbers had been enormously increased; but HMIs continued to make one annual visit to each elementary school on a prescribed day until 1895. By that time payment by results had virtually disappeared, and the elementary curriculum had been enriched by successive Codes which moved it a long way from the 1862 rigid curriculum based on the three Rs. Control of the elementary curriculum continued however until 1926, when the Regulations for elementary schools were replaced by 'suggestions'.

The 1862 Revised Code probably represented the lowest point of teacher control of the curriculum. The history of the National Union of Teachers and the professional solidarity which developed in the nineteenth century was closely associated with the battle against payment by results as a system of accountability (Tropp, 1957). By the end of the nineteenth century teachers had won the battle on that particular aspect of central influence. A gentler control of the elementary curriculum by means of regulations continued until 1926 when the regulations were abolished.

The rise of teacher control of curriculum

The 1870 Act has not, however, been universally regarded as a great step forward in popular education. It fell short of a completely secular, national system of compulsory, free education which was desired by the Chartists and many other radicals. It was described by H. G. Wells in the following way: 'Not an Act for a common universal education, it was an Act to educate the lower classes for employment on lower class lines, and with specially trained, inferior teachers.' (1934, p. 93). The control of the elementary curriculum became more important in the last quarter of the nineteenth century because there was no agreed view about what the education of the lower orders should include. As we have seen, some sections of society were concerned that elementary education should not become too good, and for them a restricted basic curriculum was a necessary part of the elementary system. In 1899 Mr Cockerton, the Auditor of the Local Government Board, suggested that rates were being spent illegally by the London School Board because they were educating element-ary-school children on curricula not provided for in the Elementary Code. The argument was that rates for education could be spent only on the kind of curricula specifically set out in the successive Codes and that anything over and above the Code curricula was strictly illegal. The judgment was made against the London School Board by the court of the Queen's Bench in 1901 and upheld by the Court of Appeal.

The Cockerton judgment had two important results: it accelerated the demand for more secondary schools (to be provided in the following year as a result of the Balfour Edu-cation Act); but it also sharpened the curricular distinction between secondary and elementary schools. It was also ensured that advanced work in elementary schools would not compete with what was still regarded as middle-class (i.e. secondary) education. This divisive view was reinforced by the 1904 Elementary Code which Eaglesham (1967) described as 'a standstill in elementary education' and as 'training for followership'. In 1926 the Elementary Regulations were abolished. The reasons for abolition, though highly political, are too complex for detailed discussion here. John White (1975) has suggested that Lord Eustace Percy's motive for abandoning the control of the curriculum by means of regula-tions was not a desire to give teachers more freedom, but a more negative reason: namely, a fear (in the year of the General Strike) that a Labour government might use their power, existing in the regulations, to control the curriculum in an explicitly socialist way. This is an extremely interesting hypothesis which deserves closer investigation, but as yet there is no conclusive evidence. Central control was, however, certainly removed in 1926 and teachers in elementary schools were from then on only restrained by a *Handbook of Sugges-tions* rather than a set of Regulations.

The Golden Age of teacher freedom

In 1944 similar freedom to determine the curriculum was given to secondary teachers, but once again the motive for this delegation of power from the centre to the teachers themselves has been questioned. John White suggests that R. A. Butler, in framing the 1944 Act, deliberately left out any requirement for the school curriculum for political reasons similar to those of Lord Eustace Percy in 1926. Tim Raison (1976) disagrees, and suggests that the neglect to make provision for regulations to continue was more likely to have been due to administrative oversight rather than political forethought. Certainly the effect was potentially of considerable importance. Until 1944 the curriculum in all secondary schools had been tightly controlled, not only by regulations but also by the fact that most pupils took the School Certificate examination. The School Certificate was a group examination requiring at least five passes including English. In effect, all secondary schools worked with a core curriculum which was established by the regulations but implemented by the structure of a group examination. There were frequent complaints about the examination as something which constrained good teaching (see the Norwood Report, 1943) but few objections to the core curriculum enshrined in the regulations.

Perhaps one reason for the disappearance of the Regulations (and the core curriculum) after 1944 was that no one at the centre knew what kind of curriculum should be offered when secondary education *for all* was introduced. It is sometimes easy to disguise ignorance and irresponsibility as freedom and generosity!

A balanced and sensible discussion of curriculum which appeared soon after the 1944 Education Act was *The Content of Education* (Council for Curriculum Reform, 1945). The case for a common curriculum for secondary schools was clearly argued, but the Council for Curriculum Reform lacked any political power base and was virtually ignored. *Laissez-faire* rather than rational planning prevailed and continued to be the curriculum philosophy for another twenty years.

Much attention, official and unofficial, was, however, paid to the highly political curricular and organisational recommendations of the Spens Report (1938) and the Norwood Report (1943). The Spens Report, on the basis of strangely misinterpreted psychological evidence, recommended that there should be three types of school with three kinds of curricula for three different categories of children: an academic curriculum for pupils in grammar schools, a more technical curriculum for those able but less theoretical pupils in secondary technical schools, and a 'practical' curriculum for the vast majority of pupils destined for secondary modern schools. The Norwood Report took this Spens argument further and 'justified' the tripartite system with different kinds of curriculum:

Types of Curriculum
In a wise economy of secondary education pupils of a particular type of mind would receive the training best suited for them and that training would lead them to an occupation where their capacities would be suitably used; that a future occupation is already present to their minds while they are still at school has been suggested, though admittedly the degree to which it is present varies. Thus, to the three main types sketched above there would correspond three main types of curriculum, which we may again attempt to indicate.

First, there would be a curriculum of which the most characteristic feature is that it treats the various fields of knowledge as suitable for coherent and systematic study for their own sake apart from immediate considerations of occupation, though at a later stage grasp of the matter and experience of the methods belonging to those fields may determine the area of choice of employment and may contribute to success in the employment chosen.

The second type of curriculum would be closely, though not wholly, directed to the special data and skills associated with a particular kind of occupation; its outlook and its methods would always be bounded by a near horizon clearly envisaged. It would thus be closely related to industry, trades and commerce in all their diversity.

20

In the third type of curriculum a balanced training of mind and body and a correlated approach to humanities, natural science and the arts would provide an equipment varied enough to enable pupils to take up the work of life: its purpose would not be to prepare for a particular job or profession and its treatment would make a direct appeal to interests, which it would awaken by practical touch with affairs.

Of the first it may be said that it may or may not look forward to University work; if it does, that is because the Universities are traditionally concerned with the pursuit of knowledge as such. Of the second we would say that it may or may not look forward to the Universities but that it should increasingly be directed to advanced studies in so far as the Universities extend their orbit in response to the demands of the technical branches of industry. (Norwood Report, 1943, p. 4)

This was a highly political doctrine disguised as scientific psychology. It served to 'guide' teachers' thinking on curriculum for many years to come. With the removal of the constraints of the Regulations after 1945 schools were free to embark upon any kind of secondary curriculum the teachers chose to offer. In 1950-1, when the group (five-subject) School Certificate examination gave way to the new General Certificate of Education single-subject Ordinary Level examination, the idea of a core curriculum or common curriculum faded away. Obsolescent Regulations and a much criticised examination system disappeared, but they were not replaced by any clear curriculum theory or any improved structure. A dangerous vacuum existed: the typical grammar-school curriculum changed very little in the post-war years; secondary-modern-school curricula, free of examination constraints, often lacked structure and purpose. They struggled to get away from the elementary tradition whilst not apeing the grammar schools, but in most cases the result was not very encouraging. Where comprehensive-school curricula developed they tended to be uncomfortable mixtures of the two traditions – elitist, grammar-school, obsolete knowledge, and elementary-school training for followership.

21

During these post-Norwood years little thought was given to the curriculum, either locally or nationally: teachers and administrators were, understandably, more concerned with pressing questions about organisation – whether to have three schools or one, how to stream or set in order to achieve good examination results. The idea that there should be no central guidance on the curriculum was reinforced by post-war Labour Ministers of Education who adopted a strange *laissez-faire* approach to this aspect of education. From 1944 to the beginning of the 1960s may therefore be seen as the Golden Age of teacher control (or non-control) of the curriculum. Maurice Kogan has also pointed out that this was the period of optimism and consensus in education: both political parties (Labour and Conservative) were committed to educational expansion, and, although there were occasional disputes, the parties were not even seriously divided until 1959 on the major issue of comprehensive secondary education. It might be said that the teachers had their chance to take control of the curriculum, but failed to take it.

The swing back to central control

By the 1960s the end of the period of educational harmony and consensus was in sight; there was a growing suspicion by teachers and LEAs that there was a desire at the centre to gain more control over the school curriculum. In 1960, David Eccles (the Conservative Minister of Education), debating the Crowther Report in the House of Commons, said that he regretted that Parliamentary debates on education were so much devoted to bricks and mortar and matters of organisation rather than the content of the curriculum. He announced his intention to 'make the Ministry's voice heard rather more often and positively and no doubt controversially'. He aimed to begin by encouraging the Ministry to carry out more educational research (Manzer, 1970). It was at this time that Eccles used the phrase 'secret garden of the curriculum' as an indication of his dislike of an important area of educational concern which seemed to be closed to public scrutiny and open discussion. Soon afterwards the Curriculum Study Group was established, which Eccles tactlessly described as a 'commando-type unit'. Teachers and LEAs were alarmed, but this was probably a 'false alarm': the Curriculum Study Group was not a body which would have become a threat to teachers. (We have this on the excellent evidence of Maurice Kogan 1978, who was at that time a civil servant at the DES, working within the Curriculum Study Group.) But professional teachers' associations as well as Local Education Authorities became increasingly hostile to the Study Group, and in 1963 the new Minister of Education, Sir Edward Boyle, decided that the Curriculum Study Group would be replaced by a more acceptable organisation. The Lockwood Committee was set up and eventually recommended that there should be a Schools Council for Curriculum and Examinations.

Since 1964 the development of the curriculum has been closely connected with the Schools Council (see Chapter 5); teacher control of the curriculum has been closely related to the power of the Schools Council. However, two features of the Council have contributed to growing dissatisfaction. First, the teachers were promised, and given, a majority on all important Schools Council committees; second, the Council adopted the policy of providing many curricular alternatives from which teachers could choose rather than formulating general policy statements about what a good school curriculum ought to contain. This 'cafeteria' approach has been a major weakness; the Council was prevented from giving guidance on an area of increasing concern – the structure and content of the curriculum as a whole.

The problems faced by the Schools Council were made more acute by the fact that criticisms of schools intensified throughout the 1960s and 1970s. These criticisms were often levelled at progressive methods and curriculum innovation, but they covered a wide range of other complaints as well. The first of the Black Papers appeared in 1969, criticising various aspects of progressive and comprehensive school policy. But that was a symptom rather than a cause of public dissatisfaction. The DES also appeared to be increasingly concerned about the question of standards in schools, and in 1974 set up the Assessment of Performance Unit (see Chapter 4). In 1976 the new Permanent Secretary at the Department of Education and Science, James Hamilton, publicly questioned the lack of attention paid to complaints made by parents and employers and criticised teachers for sheltering behind their 'expertise'. In 1976 suggestions that the curriculum was too important to be left to teachers came from moderates on the political left as well as on the right. Ann Corbett (1976) in the Fabian Society's evidence to the Taylor Committee suggested that reformed governing bodies (which should include increased representation of parents) ought to exercise more control over the curriculum.[5] Tim Raison (1976) stated that it was extremely unfortunate that the 1944 Education Act had neglected to lay down any guidelines for the curriculum. He concluded that there were strong arguments for a common curriculum in secondary schools. Teacher autonomy was under attack.

1976 was a crucial year in other matters relevant to teachers' control of the curriculum. The tenth Report of the House of Commons Expenditure Committee focused attention on the financing of education, and the lack of control that the DES appeared to have over how money was spent. The complaint was made that the DES had reduced educational planning to the banalities of resource allocation. The Tenth Report has to be seen partly as a demand that education should give value for money, but partly as a criticism of the fact that the DES appeared to condone the view that teachers alone should have control of the curriculum. In October 1976 the Prime Minister joined in this criticism of the educational *status quo*. In his speech at Ruskin College he questioned whether schools and the education service generally were doing enough to provide the industrial society with sufficient training in the basic subjects.

By the end of 1976 it was possible to identify a number of different kinds of complaints about schools and teachers under the general heading of accountability. First, financial — that the enormous education budget should be seen to be giving value for money; second, economic — that education ought to pay more attention to the needs of industry; third, parental demands loomed large — particularly in the considerations of the Taylor Committee on the composition of governing bodies of schools. As well as this there was a general swing of the pendulum against progressive methods and curricula in education, and the word 'accountability' was increasingly used in a variety of contexts and with a wide variety of meanings.

1977 was a year of even more public discussion on education. The *Auld Report* on the William Tyndale Schools was published, showing that a group of teachers had been allowed to continue far too long in what appeared to be grossly incompetent management of the curriculum;[6] the review of the Schools Council's Constitution was initiated with the explicit intention of making teachers less dominant in the Council, and less influential in the control of funds available for curriculum change. The Great Debate led eventually to the publication of the Green Paper *Education in Schools: a Consultative Document*, which hinted at a possible swing of power back to the centre in its statements about the Secretary of State not abdicating from curricular responsibilities; second, it made clear that the curriculum was not just a secret garden for teachers but was the legitimate concern of many others:

> The proper functioning of the education system in England and Wales depends on the effective cooperation of the schools, their teachers and their governors and managers; the LEAs; and the Secretaries of State in the Departments and H.M. Inspectorate. They have no intention of changing this position, which reflects the provisions of the Education Acts. At the same time they recognise the legitimate interests of others — parents, industry and commerce, for example — in the work of schools. (Para. 2 Circular 14/77)

By the end of 1978 a clear conflict of interests had emerged over the control of the curriculum, especially the secondary-school curriculum. On the one hand, teachers repeatedly declared their legitimate desire for professional autonomy; on the other hand, wider demands were made for participation and accountability in education, with special reference to the curriculum. How can such a problem of control be resolved in a democratic society? Two points need to be made immediately:

25

1   There is a political need for some kind of system of accountability which does not amount to central control of the curriculum. There must be some kind of control. The point is whether it is better for these pressures to be overt or hidden. This question will be examined in Chapters 3 and 4.
2   The second argument involves the difficult question of children's rights. If the state compels children to attend school and compels parents to send them, then the state has a corresponding duty to ensure that time is not wasted; the state has the duty of spelling out the supposed advantages of schooling and this must involve explicit statements about curriculum content.

Both of these would appear to be arguments in favour of a central influence of some kind over the curriculum. But should the influence come from the DES or from the Schools Council? These points will also be taken up in later chapters.

At the same time it should be said that teachers are quite right to be cautious about external interference in the curriculum for a number of reasons:

1   They are right to oppose the idea of a national *uniform* curriculum laid down either by the Secretary of State or by the DES (one would represent the danger of political interference, the other of bureaucratic rigidity).
2   They are right to oppose the idea of a curriculum based on lists of specific behavioural objectives.
3   They are right to fear the kind of parental interference which has occurred in some parts of the USA.
4   They are right to be suspicious of anything which might lead in the direction of some kinds of US 'evaluation' and 'accountability'.
5   They are right to resist the view of curriculum as being determined by the needs of society and especially the needs of industry.

Teachers would, however, be wrong to claim that they alone have any right to discuss the curriculum; in particular they would be wrong to suggest that individual teachers and individual schools can 'go it alone'. This is to confuse professional, *collective* autonomy with unrestrained *individual* freedom.

Having gained a good deal of curriculum control in the post-war years of educational harmony and consensus, teachers have recently lost some ground, partly as a result of increasing demands by others for participation in education and a general move in the direction of accountability. But if the secret garden of the curriculum is to be made more open, so should the secret corridors of power at the DES. This will be the main theme of the next chapter.

Summary

1 In the second half of the nineteenth century a narrow, crude form of accountability was imposed on elementary teachers: 'payment by results'.
2 Elementary teachers united in opposition to this policy, and gradually gained more freedom.
3 Elementary Regulations disappeared in 1926; Secondary Regulations were made obsolete by the 1944 Education Act.
4 Teacher freedom, already enhanced by the 1944 Act, was further increased by the replacement of the School Certificate by GCE (1951). There ceased to be any externally imposed core curriculum for secondary schools. This 'freedom' resulted in teacher non-control rather than teacher control.
5 The Curriculum Study Group (1960) was opposed by teachers, and replaced in 1964 by the Schools Council with a built-in teacher majority. Curriculum *laissez-faire* continued to prevail.
6 Since the mid-1960s, and increasingly in the 1970s, teacher 'control' of curricula has been questioned and criticised.

Chapter 3

The growing power of the mandarins and the secret service

In July 1977 Senior Chief Inspector Miss Sheila Browne made an important speech about curriculum to the Council of Local Education Authorities' Annual Conference. She subtitled her paper 'The secret garden seen by the secret service' (*Trends in Education*, 3, 1977). As with many good jokes there may be a considerable element of truth behind it: the vision of HMIs acting as secret agents on behalf of the DES mandarins was in some respects too close to the truth for comfort. Especially at a time when there is more than a slight suspicion that the DES is making a bid for increased power over the curriculum. One of the major political issues concerning the DES and curriculum control is the question of secrecy: despite the fact that open government is being urged by many prominent party politicians of the left and the right, the DES clings to the tradition of secrecy, although making occasional gestures in the direction of openness.

A word of caution may be necessary at this stage. I am not an exponent of conspiracy theory either at the DES or anywhere else: I am not suggesting that there is a tightly knit group of politically minded civil servants and HMIs who meet and formulate policy. It is reasonably well known that sometimes HMIs disagree with the mandarins, and also that both groups frequently disagree among themselves. What I am suggesting is that on many issues there is no need for a conspiracy: HMIs and civil servants, sharing similar social and educational backgrounds, tend to make the same kind of assumptions, and tend to possess similar beliefs, ideologies and obsolete theories. It is likely that DES policy, where it exists at all, is the result of that kind of 'common sense' set of shared assumptions rather than a carefully formulated theoretical viewpoint.

I will not attempt here a review of the swing of power to the centre in the mid-nineteenth century as a result of the development of a central authority in education. This has been adequately covered in Gosden (1966), Sutherland (1973) and Bishop (1971). Nor will I go over in greater detail the points made in Chapter 2 about the centre-periphery conflict 1833-1944. I will instead concentrate on the post-war years 1945-78 looking in particular at hidden DES pressures on the secondary-school curriculum.

1945-60: harmony

After the 1945 election the Labour Party had a large major-ity, and a unique opportunity to promote a new policy in education. They failed to take advantage of that chance and many would explain the failure of 1945 to 1951 by the lack of any coherent theory and policy on education. Typical of the lack of theory and lack of policy was the handling of the Ministry of Education Pamphlet *The Nation's Schools* (May 1945). This pamphlet, which had been drafted before the Labour government took office, recommended to local authorities that secondary schools should be organised on a tripartite basis, (i.e. three separate kinds of schools for three different kinds of ability — grammar, technical and modern). There were considerable protests within the Labour Party from those who supported multilateral and comprehensive schools,[1] but Ellen Wilkinson, the Minister of Education, defended the main proposals of the pamphlet even though she eventually agreed (at the June 1947 Conference) that certain passages should be re-written. Robin Pedley (1969) has suggested that the post-war Labour Ministers of Educa-tion were no match for the Ministry officials who at that time strongly favoured retaining the grammar schools and preserving their separate curriculum, whilst allowing modern schools to go their own unimportant way. This is just one example of ministers being persuaded by civil servants to carry on with a policy laid down either by a previous administration of a different political complexion or by the civil servants themselves.

There was considerable pressure both inside and outside the House of Commons to develop 'secondary education for all' in a way quite different from that set out in *The Nation's Schools*. In particular, the National Association of Labour Teachers (NALT) called for the withdrawal of the pamphlet and a reinterpretation of the 1944 Education Act in a way which would encourage the development of comprehensive schools. A House of Commons debate was opened by Margaret Herbison (a member of NALT) in March 1946, who suggested that the age of eleven was too early to make a decision about selecting children for specific kinds of education. She proposed that the only fair policy would be to have a *common* school until the legal leaving age. She also criticised the idea of parity of prestige as foolish and unworkable. She was supported in this debate by W. G. Cove, who was President of the NALT and a former President of the National Union of Teachers. He called for a withdrawal of *The Nation's Schools* and the adoption of a comprehensive secondary-school system.

Ellen Wilkinson was, however, persuaded by Ministry officials to stick to the policy laid down in *The Nation's Schools*, and to concentrate on making the tripartite system work, bolstered up by the doctrine of parity of esteem. It is difficult to believe that the highly intelligent Ministry officials at that time could really have believed that the policy of parity of esteem would ever work out in practice, but it was a convenient political slogan and Labour Ministers were persuaded to adopt this as the official Labour Party policy. *The Nation's Schools* was not withdrawn but it was not re-issued.

Ellen Wilkinson died in February 1947 and the document prepared by the Ministry of Education officials while she was Minister was later issued under the authority of the new Minister, George Tomlinson. This pamphlet, *The New Secondary Education*, was issued in June 1947. It was slightly more open on the question of comprehensive schools than *The Nation's Schools* but it still firmly interpreted the 1944 Act along tripartite lines. It is no exaggeration to say that even this new document might well have been produced by a Conservative administration at that time. The fact that two Labour Ministers of Education could be persuaded to accept the very traditional view of segregated education implicit in the document is a tribute to the capacity of the Ministry of Education civil servants for getting their own way in the face of considerable opposition within the Parliamentary Labour Party. It is probably fair to say that had the Labour Party been clearer about its own educational policy then it would have been much more difficult for the Ministry officials to prevail. But even so, it is clear that either through a continued belief in the obsolete psychology contained in the Spens Report (1938) or simply out of their own 'common sense' assumptions about what secondary education ought to be, the Ministry officials were able to put into practice a view of education which had been formulated under a previous Conservative Minister. The Ministry officials were either a generation out of date in their educational theory, or automatically more in sympathy with an elitist version of secondary education than an egalitarian comprehensive policy.

It is also remarkable that both Labour Ministers of Education took great care not to interfere with the curriculum. It was, of course, George Tomlinson who made the remark 'Minister knows nowt about curriculum.' There is as yet no evidence that Ministry officials persuaded the Labour Ministers that this must be their policy, but neither is there any evidence which shows civil servants at any stage encouraging Labour politicians to be more closely involved in the planning of the curriculum or indeed in any kind of decision-making role in curriculum matters. Tomlinson even went further and boasted of his 'neutrality' on the inevitably political issue of whether the secondary-school system ought to be tripartite or comprehensive.

1960-9 The end of consensus

By 1960, as we saw in Chapter 2, a Conservative Minister, David Eccles, wanted to reassert some central influence on

31

the curriculum. It is probably fair to say that his motives were not political in any party sense, but were motivated by what he regarded as greater educational efficiency. His actions were, however, seen as political both by teachers and by the LEAs who then combined to oppose his fairly harmless idea of a Curriculum Study Group. But was it Eccles or his civil servants who were behind the bid for more power? This we do not know, but Kogan (1978) tells us that the civil servants themselves had mixed feelings about too much power being invested in the Ministry in case future regimes were more reactionary. David Eccles's successor, Edward Boyle, climbed down and allowed the Curriculum Study Group to be replaced by the Schools Council on which teachers were to have a majority voice.

The next few years are admirably documented by Kogan (1973). Kogan's book is an excellent example of the use of carefully structured interviews to study the process of policy-making; although it is more concerned with the role of the Minister and the relationship between Ministers and civil servants than with the power and influence of the officials themselves, a number of very important insights are provided about the curriculum. In his later book, *The Politics of Curriculum Change*, 1978, Kogan refers to the 1960s as the end of the period of consensus in education; in his introduction to *The Politics of Education* (1971) he also makes the point that even in the 1950s changes had occurred which 'decisively altered the balance of power between central and local government . . . the creation of the departments Architects and Building Branch, and the control and predictive mechanisms for teacher supply, the Teacher Supply Branch, TSB' (p. 29).

A logical third measure would have been a greater degree of central influence over the curriculum, but that attempt in 1960-4 was destined to failure, possibly because it became a piece of secret service work that was 'blown' rather than an exercise in open negotiation. That story can be told elsewhere: here we are concerned with the strength of influence wielded by civil servants in secret whilst declaring in public that they have little or no power (and sometimes no knowledge of education). It is interesting that Kogan clearly attributes more power to the civil servants than either Boyle or Crosland were willing to admit existed:[2]

> As Crosland says, an Under-Secretary put forward many of the fourteen points on teacher supply which he advocated ministerially. Under-Secretaries, and their subordinates, are thus policy-makers, though in each of these examples nothing could have happened without ministerial sanctioning. . . . Most civil servants are like most ministers – inadequate to fully exploit the potentialities of their role. But, in the view of this former administrator, the literature makes far too many concessions to ministerial narcissism. The ability of even the most able minister to create, promote and carry out policies is limited.
>
> One senior civil servant at Education with whom I have discussed this point said that 'I can honestly say that there is not one new policy in my sector of responsibility that I have not either started or substantially contributed to over the last twenty years'. (Boyle and Crosland, *The Politics of Education*, 1971, p. 41).

It is also important to emphasise that Kogan chose to study two exceptionally able and powerful Ministers; had he picked a more 'average' pair of Ministers, then the power of the civil servants might have appeared to have been even more startling. (What a pity no one ever documented the story of Wilkinson and Tomlinson using the same methods!) Kogan described both Crosland and Boyle as 'unusually gifted', and pointed out that Crosland had specifically prepared himself for office by his own writing:

> Few Ministers can or do prepare themselves in this way. When they don't, the Department will have its 'own' policies to continue and refine and prepare. There is also disjunction between the time scales of politics and of policy formulation. Crosland says, 'I reckon it takes you six months to get your head properly above water, a year to get the general drift of most of the field, and two years really to master the whole of a Department' (*The Politics of Education*, p. 43).

The whole book should be read and re-read carefully, (perhaps in conjunction with the Crossman Diaries, H. Thomas, 1968 and L. Chapman, 1978) as a means of getting closer to an understanding of the part really played by civil servants in educational policy. One example must be sufficient here:

> Crosland was troubled with uncertainty about the proposal to create two parallel systems of higher education (the binary system) and he criticises civil servants for forcing a decision too early on him. The decision to create thirty polytechnics was not at all in line with the Labour Party's Taylor Committee recommendations of a few years earlier to create a large and undifferentiated system of higher education (*The Politics of Education*, p. 52).

OECD Report on DES 1976

Such manipulation of Ministers by civil servants can take place only when the prevailing atmosphere is one of secrecy. Secrecy was one of the main criticisms of the DES made in a Report by a party of distinguished visitors from the OECD who had been commissioned to review the work of the DES in 1976.[3] They begin by pointing out the difference between the formal position of the DES and the reality: 'At the start one is confronted by the position of the DES in the web of organisations and agencies that have educational responsibilities in the U.K. *It is true to say both that it has extremely limited authority and that it has great powers* (author's italics).

Our civil servants are praised for their 'discipline, fidelity and morale' and it is noted with approval that they are 'chosen for their individual merits, not their political allegiance'. But there are, suggests the Report, corresponding disadvantages:

> A permanent officialdom possessing such external protections and internal disciplines becomes a power in its own right. A British Department composed of professional civil servants who have watched the Ministers come and go is an entity that only an extremely foolish or powerful politician will persistently challenge or ignore.

The prestige, acquaintanceships, and natural authority of leading civil servants give them a standing in the civil forum often superior to that of their de jure political superiors. They are, in the continental phrase, *notables* whose opinions must be given special weight, whether or not votes in the next election will be affected.

This power is compounded by the tradition of secrecy enshrined in the official Secrets Act which covers virtually everything that even the most junior civil servant does.

The habits of British government preclude letting down the bars of confidentiality, but it cannot be doubted that groups outside the Department believe that departmental decision-making is not conducted sufficiently in the open, and, moreover, that secrecy at central levels may impair the coordination between central and local administration.

The separation of the planning process from other forms of supervision and control is also worthy of note. No standing committee of Parliament exists to which the Department reports. Nor are there formal institutions of consultation requiring officers of the Department regularly to exchange views with the various constituencies affected by their plans or to defend their decision against criticism. Where basic questions of the plan are concerned, the principle means of consultation are informal, and are largely determined by the Department's views of its needs.

The particular task of the OECD experts was to examine as a piece of policy-making the 1972 White Paper *Education: A Framework for Expansion*. One of their criticisms was the lamentable neglect of the 16-19 age group. This might be another example of the tendency for policy-making to arise out of values, assumptions and experience; the plight of 16-19-year-olds not in sixth forms at school is remote from the experience of most senior civil servants. Once again it is important to stress that the kind of bias referred to is not (necessarily) the result of a deliberate plot, but simply of an incomplete view of reality. A limited perception of educational needs (as well as educational theory) is combined with a civil servant's natural inclination to 'play safe':

The chief features of the bases for its policy formation seemed to be characterised by attempts to: minimise the degree of controversiality in the planning process and its results; reduce possible alternatives to matters of choice of resource allocation; limit the planning process to those parts of the educational services and functions strictly controlled by the DES; exploit as fully as possible the powers, prerogatives and responsibilities given to the DES under the 1944 Education Act; under-state as much as possible the full role of the government in the determination of the future course of educational policy and even minimise it in the eyes of the general public.

The preservation of this powerful position, by combining the task of coherent planning with defensive tactics, excluding an open planning process, public hearings or, even, participation, seems to an outside observer as a mixture of strength and weakness.

**Expenditure Committee Report
'policy-making in the DES' (1976)**

During 1975-6 the DES was also subjected to the scrutiny of another group of critics: the House of Commons Expenditure Committee, which made a general study of policy-making in the DES. The two major complaints of the Education Sub-Committee were that the DES was excessively secretive and that it lacked an adequate planning organisation. Ironically the Committee itself suffered from this secretiveness when DES officials refused to make available the planning and analysis review papers on which educational policies had been based! As with the OECD Report, the Expenditure Committee suggested that the DES tended to reduce policy-making to the level of resource allocation rather than to indulge in long-term planning. One interesting recommendation was that a permanent standing education commission should be set up, having the authority and resources to contribute an independent view on strategic educational planning for the whole educational service with a membership which would include trade unions, employers and ordinary citizens.

It should be noted that the DES has failed to respond either to the OECD or to the Expenditure Committee Reports on the question of secrecy. Their response to the Expenditure Committee was extremely curt: a thirteen-page document mainly consisting of action already being taken, implying that the Committee really did not know what it was talking about.

The Yellow Book (1976)

We pass now from external allegations of secrecy and ineffective planning at the DES to questions of curriculum, and a specific example of the DES in operation. The initiative for the confidential production of the Yellow Book came from the Prime Minister, James Callaghan, possibly on the advice of Bernard Donaghue (Kogan, 1978, pp. 64-5). A more doubtful version of the story attributes the Prime Minister's concern about educational standards to his daughter's decision to send her much publicised children to independent schools. The reasons are, in any case, less important than the outcome. Fred Mulley, briefly Secretary of State for Education in 1975, was asked to produce a report on standards, and the Yellow Book was the result, details from which were eventually leaked to the press in 1976 before the Prime Minister's October speech at Ruskin College. The DES had been asked to comment on four areas of public concern about education:

1 The teaching of the three Rs in primary schools
2 The curriculum for comprehensive schools
3 The examination system
4 The 16-19 age group.

I will consider 1 and 2 in this chapter but leave 3 for the later chapter on examinations. On primary teaching, the Yellow Book reviews the 'child-centred' approach and is, on balance, critical of the teaching profession in this respect:

In the hands of a skilled teacher this 'child-centred' approach can greatly advance the learning process for large numbers of children, although it can also have adverse

37

consequences if not applied with adequate understanding and skill. For success, teaching of a high quality is needed, with careful planning and a clear understanding of aims. There are signs that it is becoming more widely understood that the new approaches do demand rigour and some recognition of the widely varying capabilities of individual teachers. (para. 27)

This would have been an unexceptionable verdict if it had been made by anyone other than the DES, in secret, to the Prime Minister, but, as many teachers were quick to point out, the profession as a whole was being criticised for carrying out precisely those policies which had been encouraged as almost official doctrine for many years in DES publications as well as by HMIs on their courses and visits to schools. It might be added that just as child-centred primary education had been officially fostered on the basis of totally inadequate research, now it was being criticised on equally poor evidence.

The sections in the Yellow Book on the secondary curriculum are equally open to criticism. After years of ignoring the problem of lack of structure and balance in the secondary curriculum (see chapter 2), the DES suddenly appeared to be converted to the notion of a common core curriculum. But the level of argument here is extremely low; no justification is given for statements about what ought to be in the curriculum (such as modern languages); and no theoretical discussion of the nature of knowledge was even attempted or referred to. Moreover, by failing to make elementary distinctions between such terms as 'core curriculum', 'common curriculum', 'uniform curriculum' and 'compulsory curriculum', the DES inevitably engaged the teachers' unions in conflict as soon as the secret document became public – either deliberately or accidentally.

Once again the combination of secrecy with poor research and lack of long-term planning characterised DES policy. It almost guaranteed failure in this most important aspect of comprehensive school policy.

The Prime Minister's Ruskin Speech (1976)

When the Prime Minister eventually made his speech at Ruskin College on 18 October 1976, it was regarded as a great anti-climax. The critical sections of the Yellow Book which would have given considerable offence to the teaching profession (and those on the Schools Council, see Chapter 5) were cut out or watered down. The speech came across as a sensible, not very controversial statement about education in a changing industrial society; the only criticism that might be made was that the Prime Minister leaned too far in the direction of seeing education as a means of servicing the manpower needs of industry. More importantly, the speech served to launch the so-called Great Debate on Education 1976-7.

The Great Debate

One verdict of many of those involved was that it was not a debate and it was not very great. It was, however, a useful public discussion about education. Launched by the Prime Minister in October 1976, it continued with a DES background paper to be discussed at a number of regional conferences in the spring of 1977. The DES background paper was interesting for a number of reasons. First, as an example of agenda-setting; second, as a nice instance of slightly changing the direction of the debate to suit the DES book. The Prime Minister had raised questions about four issues: (1) The three Rs in primary schools, (2) comprehensive curriculum, (3) examinations, (4) 16-19 age groups; but the agenda now became: (1) curriculum 5 to 16; (2) the assessment of standards; (3) the education and training of teachers; (4) school and working life. The background paper, 'Educating Our Children', became available after preliminary consultations with educational and industrial organisations in November and December 1976. By the time the February and March regional conferences were held the agenda had thus become a series of focused questions using the text of 'Educating Our Children' as background.

Educating our Children
Four Subjects for Debate
Questions for discussion at the Regional Conferences in
England during February and March 1977.

The school curriculum, 5-16
1 The fundamental requirement is to meet the needs and
reasonable aspirations of pupils and the needs of the
country. The problem is to ensure the coverage of certain
essentials without stifling the initiatives of teachers,
preventing innovation or making education unduly narrow.
Two major questions arise:
> (i) What should be the aims and content of a core
> curriculum?
> (ii) How best can an agreed core curriculum be put into
> effect?

(See paragraphs 2.1 – 2.18 of conference paper *Educating
our Children*)

The assessment of standards
2 To assess the quality of the education children are
receiving we need to know:
> (i) how individual pupils are progressing in the acquisi-
> tion of basic skills and more generally;
> (ii) how the school system as a whole is performing.

Do we have adequate means of obtaining reliable information about the performance of pupils and schools and if
not what further measures are required?
(See paragraphs 3.1 – 3.27 of conference paper *Educating
our Children*)

The education and training of teachers
3 Whatever consensus might emerge on the ways to tackle
some or all of the problems listed above, we shall not
improve school education unless the teachers are
committed to what needs to be done and equipped
with the necessary skills.
We need to consider:
> (i) what steps can be taken to ensure that all teachers
> receive the in-service training and education they
> need at the various stages of their careers;

40

(ii) the academic and professional requirements of
teachers which need to be provided for in their
initial training and in particular the implications
these have for entrance requirements.
(See paragraphs 4.1 – 4.11 of conference paper *Educating
our Children*)

School and working life
4   Children growing up in an industrial society need to
understand it, and to appreciate the dependence of our
living standards on the creation and production of goods
and services. Those engaged in industry are often critical
of the schools on the grounds that basic skills have been
neglected, and that insufficient pupils pursue studies in
science and mathematics; nor are the most able attracted
to manufacturing industries. Those engaged in education
are critical of industry, on the grounds that most people in
industry show little interest in the schools and that education at all levels does not receive as much support as it
should from the employers.

A reasonable grasp of English and mathematics is essential to children in both their working and their personal
lives. Education must provide these skills while stimulating
pupils to acquire further knowledge and to enrich their
lives by an appreciation of the creative and artistic achieve-
ments of mankind.
Two major questions arise:
(i) How best can children be educated towards an
awareness and understanding of our technological
and industrial society and of their own role within it?
(ii) How can employers make the best use of school
leavers and what contribution can industry make to
education?
(See paragraphs 5.1 – 5.10 of conference paper *Educating
our Children*)

As might have been predicted, no clear guidance emerged
as a result of the regional conferences in the Great Debate. If
this was the response of the DES to OECD and the Expenditure Committee to indulge in more open consultation then it
was almost completely unsatisfactory.

The Green Paper (July 1977)

The next stage in the agenda setting was the publication of the long-awaited Green Paper *Education in Schools: A Consultative Document*. This was presented to Parliament in July 1977. It was rumoured that the consultative document had been drafted and re-drafted many times (even more than is usually the case for a Green Paper). Attempts had been made to mollify the teachers' unions: questions about the core curriculum, for example, had been rendered almost innocuous (and therefore almost meaningless). Once again the Prime Minister's Ruskin speech with its Yellow Book background served to focus attention and set the agenda:

1.1 In his speech at Ruskin College, Oxford on 18th October 1976 the Prime Minister called for a public debate on education. The debate was not to be confined to those professionally concerned with education, but was to give full opportunity for employers and trade unions, and parents, as well as teachers and administrators, to make their views known.

1.2 The speech was made against a background of strongly critical comment in the press and elsewhere on education and educational standards. Children's standards of performance in their school work were said to have declined. The curriculum, it was argued, paid too little attention to the basic skills of reading, writing, and arithmetic, and was over-loaded with fringe subjects. Teachers lacked adequate professional skills, and did not know how to discipline children or to instil in them concern for hard work or good manners. Underlying all this was the feeling that the educational system was out of touch with the fundamental need for Britain to survive economically in a highly competitive world through the efficiency of its industry and commerce.

1.3 Some of these criticisms are fair. There is a wide gap between the world of education and the world of work. Boys and girls are not sufficiently aware of the importance of industry to our society, and they are not taught much about it. In some schools the curriculum has been over-loaded, so that basic skills of literacy and numeracy, the building blocks of education, have been neglected. A small minority of schools has simply failed to provide an adequate education by modern standards. More frequently, schools have been over-ambitious, introducing modern languages without sufficient staff to meet the needs of a much wider range of pupils, or embarking on new methods of teaching mathematics without making sure the teachers understood what they were teaching, or whether it was appropriate to the pupils' capacities or the needs of their future employers.

Without admitting that the DES and HMI have been neglectful in the past, there is a series of indications that a new positive approach (especially on the curriculum) was to be a characteristic of future policy:

> The national level: the Secretaries of State are responsible in law for the promotion of education of the people of England and Wales. They need to know what is being done by LEAs and, through them, what is happening in the schools. They must draw attention to national needs if they believe the education system is not adequately meeting them.

This message of strengthened participation by the DES is put even more forcibly in the section on the curriculum:

> 2.19 It would not be compatible with the duty of the Secretaries of State to 'promote the education of the people of England and Wales', or with their accountability to Parliament, to abdicate from leadership on educational issues which have become a matter of lively public concern. The Secretaries of State will therefore seek to establish a broad agreement with their partners in the education service on a framework for the curriculum, and, particularly, on whether, because there are aims common to all schools and to all pupils at certain stages, there should be a 'core' or 'protected part'.

LEAs are also nudged into taking a more active part in curriculum planning:

43

2.20 LEAs must coordinate the curriculum and its development in their own areas, taking account of local circumstances, consulting local interests and drawing on the work
of the Schools Council and other curricular research and
development agencies.

We are then told of the next step:

The Secretaries of State propose to invite the local authority and teachers' associations to take part in early consultations about the conduct of a review of curricular arrangements in each local authority area. . . . The intention . . .
is that . . . they should issue a Circular asking all LEAs to
carry out a review in their own areas in consultation with
their teachers and to report the results within about twelve
months.

The NUT and others (as well as LEAs) might object to being
told what to do in the form of a common core curriculum,
but surely no one could object to informing the DES about
what they were already doing? The agenda for that exercise
are set out in DES Circular 14/77.

**DES Circular 14/77: 'LEA Arrangements for the
School Curriculum'**

This Circular is at once fairly demanding in the kind of
information sought, and at the same time reassuring the other
two partners (LEAs and teachers) as well as the Schools
Council that no takeover bid is intended. The relevant sections
of the annex to the Circular are quoted in full below:

*A. Local arrangements for the co-ordination of
School Curricula and any plans for development*
A1 What procedures have the authority established to
enable them to carry out their curricular responsibilities
under Section 23 of the Education Act 1944?
A2 What systematic arrangements, if any, have the authority established for the collection of information about the
curricula offered by schools in their area?

44

A3 How do the authority, where appropriate, develop policy on matters relating to school curricula? In particular, what part is played in making and carrying out such policy by (i) local authority inspectors or advisers, (ii) teachers?

A4 How do the authority arrange for governors and managers of schools to play a part in curricular matters?

A5 What support do the authority offer to schools wishing to engage in curricular initiatives or to adopt new curricula ideas, including those deriving from Schools Council work, in terms of (a) advisory services, (b) financial aid, (c) in-service training, (d) other help?

A6 What local curriculum development work have the authority initiated since January 1974?

A7 What steps have the authority taken to help schools comply, so far as curriculum is concerned, with the provisions and intentions of the Sex Discrimination Act 1975?

B. Curricular balance and breadth

B1 How do the authority help schools decide on the relative emphasis they should give to particular aspects of the curriculum, especially the promotion of literacy and numeracy?

B2 How do the authority help primary schools make appropriate provision for pupils who by the age of 8 have made relatively slow progress in learning to read and write or to use number?

B3 What contribution have the authority made to the consideration of the problem faced by secondary schools, of providing suitable subject options for older pupils while avoiding the premature dropping of curricular elements regarded as essential for all pupils?

B4 What curricular elements do the authority regard as essential?

B5 How do the authority help secondary schools provide for (i) moral education, (ii) health education, (iii) careers education, (iv) social education through community links, etc whilst giving adequate attention to the basic educational skills? What part is played by the idea of a core or protected part of the curriculum?

B6 How do the authority help schools promote racial understanding?

B7 What kind of help do the authority give secondary schools with the planning of sixth form curricula? Is there a policy for the provision for minority subjects, for example within groups of schools or within an area?
B8 What special provision do the authority make for children whose mother tongue is not English?

C. Particular subject areas
A number of points need to be made on the stance adopted by the DES (and probably HMI) regarding this Circular:

1 It goes far beyond what might have been expected from the original Green Paper
2 Section B might be seen in terms of a strong (but disguised) push in the direction of a common curriculum
3 The inclusion of a special section on modern languages might encourage LEAs and schools to devote more resources to that area
4 All of this without benefit of any kind of theoretical justification or long-term planning research base.

HMI Document: 'Curriculum 11-16', December 1977

It was stated earlier that there have been occasions when the DES and HMI have had minor if not profound disagreements. There was, however, little sign of such conflict in the period 1976-8. The discussion document 'Curriculum 11-16' produced by HMI, after many years work, should be seen in the general context of the Great Debate, the Green Paper and the Curriculum Review. 'Foreword. These papers have been overtaken by events and it is important that neither their content nor their purpose should be misunderstood.' A necessary cautionary note, because whereas the Green Paper takes care not to antagonise teachers' unions, the HMI who had been working on this document over a period of years come out firmly in favour of a common curriculum, although they state that:

There is no intention anywhere in the papers which follow

of advocating a centrally controlled or directed curriculum; nevertheless if the questions which are proposed are regarded as valid, all who are concerned professionally with education, and above all teachers themselves, have an obligation to seek answers and to work out the consequences.

Section 1 of the document argues the case for a common curriculum, and, incidentally, is highly critical of the option system which is typical of the 14-16 age group's curriculum in so many schools. They argue that education should be a right, and that the typical arrangement of options in secondary schools, far from giving pupils freedom, may prevent their right of access to certain kinds of knowledge. It is rather unfortunate that no acknowledgment is given to J. P. White in this context since the argument is almost entirely his.

A distinction is also made between a *common* curriculum and a *core* curriculum (p. 5). The basis of the common curriculum is to be eight 'areas of experience' which are assumed to be sensible but not justified in any way. The strictures the HMI employ about an extended common curriculum might well apply to their own check-list: 'Some schools are consciously moving towards an enlarged common curriculum, by extending, for example, the central core of compulsory subjects to include some form of science and/or social studies and/or health education. Such curriculum construction in terms of subjects is acceptable when, but only when, everyone is clear what is to be achieved through them' (p. 6).

The suggested check-list is as follows:

Areas of Experience: the aesthetic and creative
the ethical
the linguistic
the mathematical
the physical
the scientific
the social and political
the spiritual

Section 2 is concerned with 'schools and society'; section 3 is about 'schools and preparation for work'. The rest of the document is made up of specialist contributions by various

47

groups of HMI in subject committees. These, unfortunately, do not completely fit in with the theoretical outline contained in Section 1, but nevertheless include some sensible general views about curriculum development. Other contributions go a long way towards spelling out the essential core, of knowledge and skills for specific subjects. 'Curriculum 11-16' is a useful discussion document but falls short of what might be regarded as a finished policy document for curriculum planning. Just as the DES (according to OECD) reduce educational planning to questions of resource allocation, so HMI tend to reduce curriculum planning to the banalities of timetabling. The final sections of 'Curriculum 11-16' which deal with staffing and timetabling are much more professional than most of the rest of the document (although it must be said that some of sections on specialist subjects are excellent).

'Curriculum 11-16' is certainly a step in the right direction, but it might be open to misuse. The problem is that this discussion document from HMI plus the Curriculum Review, plus the APU on the horizon could encourage schools to move into a style of curriculum planning and evaluation which has proved disastrous in the USA; the behavioural objectives model of curriculum, and performance – based methods of evaluation and accountability. (See chapter 7 on the 'Politics of evaluation' for a discussion of why this move would be so disastrous.) Meanwhile a group of HMI have moved into action in a number of LEAs, studying the operation of the common curriculum in practice.

Conclusion

The two major criticisms of the DES have been secrecy and ineffective planning.[4] There is little sign of real progress regarding 'openness', despite the Great Debate; but there are many signs that the DES under James Hamilton, and HMI under Sheila Browne will wish to take a more central and influential part in curriculum planning and development. Unfortunately it may be the case that this influence will not be entirely beneficial: having moved away from the Scylla of *laissez-faire* the DES shows no sign of possessing an adequate theoretical base for curriculum change and is in danger of getting too close to the Charybdis of behaviouristic, mechanistic approaches to curriculum and evaluation. It may also be no coincidence that the Treasury appears to favour such objectives planning approaches. It has even been suggested that money was diverted away from the DES towards the Manpower Services Commission because they were even more amenable to such behaviouristic planning than the DES. The next chapter will describe one specific example of this 'new look': the Assessment of Performance Unit.

Clearly there is a need for a national policy on the whole curriculum. That is not the issue: what is being questioned is whether the best means of initiating such a policy is secrecy and deceit or open negotiation.

Summary

1   The DES, in common with the British civil service as a whole, tends to operate by stealth and secrecy.
2   DES officials have probably been more influential than ministers in some policy decisions, including curricular decisions.
3   DES secrecy has been condemned by OECD and the House of Commons Expenditure Committee.
4   A recent example of secrecy and manipulation was the 1976 Yellow Book.
5   The Great Debate has not served to open up the real questions about the curriculum.
6   There are a number of signs, such as Circular 14/77 and 'Curriculum 11-16', that there is a desire to gain more central control of the curriculum.

Chapter 4

The Assessment of Performance Unit

Introduction

Chapter 3 argued that a major characteristic of the DES was a tendency to operate by stealth rather than by open discussion of policy and policy changes. We have also seen that there is evidence of a move in recent years by the DES/HMI alliance to take on a much more positive role in curriculum matters.

I suggest that one manifestation of this new role is the development of the Assessment of Performance Unit (APU) which was set up by the DES in 1974 but planned some years before that by HMI and DES. Part of the purpose of this chapter will be to set down the known facts about the origin and development of the APU. But, since I am suggesting that there may be more to the APU than meets the eye at first glance, it will also be necessary to look closely at how the development of the APU may have changed from the original declared intention. It will also be necessary to look closely at the stated aims of the APU, and to judge what is likely to happen in the future on the basis of trends already emerging.

The origin of the APU

The intention to form a unit concerned with the assessment of performance of school pupils was mentioned by Reg Prentice, at that time a Labour MP and the Secretary of State for Education, in a speech to the National Association of Schoolmasters' Conference in April 1974. An official announcement about the APU came soon afterwards (August 1974) in the White Paper *Educational Disadvantage and the Educational Needs of Immigrants* (Cmnd 5720). This White Paper was the response by the DES to the Report on Education by a House of Commons Select Committee on Race Relations and Immigration.

It is very likely that the APU, or something like it, was being planned several years before the Race Relations Report was published, but the DES would have realised that any proposal to monitor standards nationally would have been strongly resisted by the teaching profession. To assess the special needs of disadvantaged children, however, is much less offensive professionally, and might even be regarded as highly laudable, so it must have been very tempting for DES officials who wanted to introduce a national testing programme to wrap it up as part of a programme for the disadvantaged, and set it up alongside the Educational Disadvantage Unit (EDU).

At this point, it will be useful to look at the terms of reference of the APU, partly to see how appropriate they were in the 1974 context, and partly to see how they may have been interpreted more recently.

The terms of reference of the APU are to promote the development of methods of assessing and monitoring the achievement of children at school, and to seek to identify the incidents of under-achievement.

The tasks laid down are:
1   To identify and appraise existing instruments and methods of assessment which may be relevant for these purposes.
2   To sponsor the creation of new instruments and techniques for assessment, having due regard to statistical and sampling methods.
3   To promote the conduct of assessment in cooperation with Local Education Authorities and teachers.
4   To identify significant differences of achievement related to the circumstances in which children learn, including the incidence of under-achievement, and to

make the findings available to those concerned with resource allocation within the department, LEAs and schools.

It would seem fair to say that few (outside the DES) would have predicted the way the APU has developed from its particular origin in Educational Disadvantage and those particular terms of reference. A low profile has been kept, and the rumblings of discontent have been brushed aside.

The first indication that the APU was to have a much wider role than catering for the educational disadvantaged probably came from an article by Brian Kay in *Trends in Education*, 2, 1975. It is an excellent article: lucid, persuasive and generally sensible, but it contains no reference at all to the EDU or even to disadvantaged children. The emphasis, set in the first paragraph, is on *standards*, and anxiety about standards:

> In recent years there has been a growing interest in the assessment of pupils' performance at school, related in the minds of many people to some anxiety about standards. This interest and concern is felt not only by teachers but by politicians and administrators, employers and the general public.

The other main theme of the article was to stress that the curriculum should be seen not in terms of subjects but in terms of skills and knowledge. In order to look at pupils' performance across the curriculum in a non-subject way six kinds of development were hypothesised.

Verbal
Mathematical
Scientific
Ethical
Aesthetic
Physical

The six kinds of development, later changed slightly, were defined as follows:

1   Verbal — communication through reading, writing, listening and speaking in a wide range of modes to suit the

occasion, the purpose and the subject matter. This is perhaps self-evidently the line of development to which every
subject in the curriculum can contribute, and on which
every subject depends.

2   Mathematical – communication through number,
graph, model and diagram. The range of subjects which
contribute to this (or which depend upon this) is less than
the first, but still includes all which are concerned at any
time with the non-verbal communication of concepts of
quantity or relation.

3   Scientific – observation, the selection, evaluation and
use of evidence, testing of hypotheses, the use of experiment. While verbal and mathematical development is
concerned with forms of communication, this is more
a matter of technique and approach. It is equally relevant to history and geography and to chemistry or
physics.

4   Ethical – the pupil's understanding of himself, his
development as a responsible person, his sensitivity to
other people and his moral attitude towards his environment. This again forms an element in most parts of the
curriculum. Religious education, history, literature perhaps in particular offer a fruitful context, though science
and geography have a part to play; drama, debate and the
analytical essay are among the techniques used to explore
and deepen it. The general life and organisation of school
are significant for this as for some of the other lines of
development.

5   Aesthetic – the pupil's appreciation of form, colour,
texture, sound; his affective response to his environment,
his respect for quality, his capacity to harness imagination
and feeling in creative work. This, like the ethical field, is
self-evidently concerned both with mind and feeling. Again,
it forms an element which can hardly be excluded from
any part of the curriculum without aridity. It is certainly
to be found in mathematics and science as well as, more
obviously, in the creative arts.

6   Physical – the pupil's developing muscular control, his ability to use his body efficiently and expressively. This involves a range of physical skills, from those needed by the pre-school child when he first starts to use a pencil to the sensitive handling of scientific apparatus, the use of paint brush, scalpel or chisel, and the use of movement and dance in communication.

Kay is careful to make all sorts. of qualifications about these six 'roughly identifiable areas', but they become the basic structure for the monitoring programme, except that 'ethical' was later modified to become 'social and personal'. There are, of course, a number of epistemological and educational difficulties in accepting this list of six areas of development, but that is not our purpose here. Some of these problems, as well as the statistical difficulties will be considered briefly towards the end of this chapter.

Trends in Education is not a journal which is very widely read by the teaching profession. The low profile of the APU was maintained after the appearance of the Brian Kay article, but the lines of development were now firmly established. A few inconsistencies of argument appeared which were to become more serious later. Little more was said about the APU throughout 1975 and 1976. In 1976 an interesting reference was made to the APU in the Yellow Book. Since the Yellow Book is still regarded as a secret document and is, therefore, not generally available, I will quote in full:

52   The APU was set up as recently as August 1974 (Command 5720). Its start was slow, partly because of suspicion in some quarters of the teaching profession (the NUT in particular) and partly because of delay in finding a chairman for its consultative committee. This committee which is widely representative of educational interests, has now met under Professor Barry Supple of Sussex University. Otherwise the Unit itself is a small group within the DES under the leadership of a Staff Inspector, with a share of the Department's research budget at its disposal. It will work largely by commissioning outside projects and is supported by a coordinating group and several specialist sub-groups drawn partly from the Department and

Inspectorate and partly from outside.

53   The terms of reference of the Unit as set out in the White Paper are as follows . . . [already quoted in full on p. 55.]

54   The Unit is now engaged in the first of these tasks. In terms of the curriculum the priorities are to follow up the recommendations of the Bullock Report about the testing of reading and the use of language, to evaluate and pursue the reports on testing mathematical aptitude (TAMS) previously commissioned by the Department through its research budget, and to make a start in considering the assessment of science. Thereafter it will turn its attention to other areas of the curriculum.

It may again be significant that no mention is made of the disadvantaged. It also seems strange to explain the delay in the work of the Unit in terms of the difficulty of finding a chairman for the consultative committee: could it be that it was regarded as preferable for the 'small group within the DES' to get on with the work without the embarrassment of a consultative group while the main thrust of the work of the Unit was being settled? Certainly the membership of the consultative committee was not announced until 4 February 1976 (long after Brian Kay's definitive article was written). (See Appendix 1 for the list of members of the consultative committee at that time.)

During 1977 the APU appeared to be accepted as part of the educational scene; references to it, and documents about it, began to proliferate. In January 1977 the DES issued 'a programme of work' again written by Brian Kay, the Staff Inspector in charge of the Unit at that time. This is an extremely useful document since it looks at each of the four tasks and elaborates on what will be involved in their achievement:

1   To identify and appraise existing instruments and methods of assessment which may be relevant for these purposes.

To do this, subject specialists and measurements experts will review existing tests and identify new methods (including those developed by curriculum development evaluators and Examining Boards).

2 To sponsor the creation of new instruments and techniques for assessment, having due regard to statistical and sampling methods.

Before new instruments could be developed prior research would be necessary: the specification of such research was 'one of the main tasks of the Unit during the first two years'. Appropriate statistical and sampling methods would have to be found.

3 To promote the conduct of assessment in cooperation with LEAs and teachers.

Monitoring implies the sampling of educational outcomes by assessing the performance of a small number of pupils. The intention would be to show trends in the levels of pupils' performance over a number of years as well as to 'measure the degree of response of the educational system to the changing needs of society'. (It is by no means clear what that means!) 'In addition to national monitoring, it is likely that the APU will make the assessment materials developed through its agency available (with suitable safeguards) to other users, such as LEAs. . . .' (this extension of light-sampling monitoring to possible blanket testing by LEAs is one of the dangers which some educationists find extremely alarming[1]).

4 To identify significant differences of achievement related to the circumstances in which children learn, including the incidence of under-achievement, and to make the findings available to those concerned with resource allocation within the Department, LEAs and schools.

National monitoring may be supplemented by 'in depth' studies to show relationships between social and educational factors and pupils' performance. The information thus obtained about groups of pupils and different curricula could be used as a basis for policy, including resource allocation.

Two points need to be made about the document summarised above: First, once again no mention is made of the disadvantaged, despite task 4 and it is by no means clear what kind of 'in depth' studies would be needed to make the work obtained from the massive APU budget relevant to the disadvantaged. Second, the shift towards monitoring standards away from diagnosing individual pupil's difficulties has been carried much further and to an extent which many would find disturbing.

At about the same time as Kay's programme of work was published there also appeared from the DES 'Educating Our Children'. One of the four subjects to be included in the Great Debate was 'the assessment of standards' and a brief but significant reference to the APU is made in 'Educating Our Children':

3.12   The recognition that further work was needed on sampling standards led to the establishment in 1974 of the Assessment of Performance Unit within the DES. The Unit consists of a small central team and a number of professional working groups; a coordinating group and those for mathematics, English and science have already been established. A Consultative Committee, which represents a wide range of educational interests, considers the proposals made by the working group and advises on them.

3.13   The introduction of a national system of assessment requires decisions on such issues as: what, in each chosen area of the curriculum, should be assessed, and at what ages; and what sampling system should be chosen so as to ensure reliable results in sufficient detail without undue disruption to the work of the school. These matters and other necessary preparatory work are now receiving attention from the APU and from the many interests within and related to the education service concerned with the development of policy, with the aim of starting on a programme of national assessment in 1978.

No mention is made of the origin of the APU; the justification is now blatantly in terms of standards.

Later in 1977 (May) C. H. Selby, HMI produced a document 'APU — Questions and Answers' as a useful guide for anyone asked to speak about the APU (presumably members of the Consultative Committee as well as the working groups). Question 14 of this document is particularly interesting: 'How will wash-back effect be avoided?' (One of the fears expressed by those who thought that the APU would inevitably have a controlling effect on the content of the curriculum.) The answer to Question 14:

> Teachers have a traditional love-hate relationship with external examination systems. They value an independent judgment and stimulus but they resent some of the influences on classroom activities. The testing proposed by the APU will rely on light sampling which will involve individual pupils and school relatively infrequently, say once every five to ten years. It should be possible to avoid heavy sampling with such frequency that teachers will be tempting to 'teach to the test'. In any case since individual pupils, teachers, schools and LEAs will not be identified in the statements made as a result of the national monitoring, there will be no cause for competition and the training for the test that this can often encourage. On the other hand monitoring can have a beneficial effect long-term in the sense that if we monitor things regarded by a large number of people as important this will help ensure that society's priorities are reflected appropriately in school curricula. Given the broad conception of testing the lines of pupil development there will undoubtedly be far-reaching discussions about the school curriculum when the results of the monitoring begin to be published.

This seems to be having it both ways: we might be forgiven for summarising the answer as: 'There will be no wash-back; any wash-back that does occur will be very good wash-back.'

Question 19 is also very enlightening: 'How soon will LEAs be able to relate their own monitoring to that of the APU?' (Another familiar fear or desire is that APU testing will legitimise 'blanket testing' of an undesirable kind by LEAs. This was one of the NUT's early worries.) Answer to Question 19:

> Monitoring by LEAs is at a very early stage. Few have started monitoring. A much larger group are actively

discussing monitoring procedures. The NFER have been asked by some LEAs to produce new tests standardised for their own pupils. There is obvious advantage in these tests being very similar to those being developed for the APU. Results from LEAs using existing, well-established, tests for monitoring may be difficult to compare with APU findings.

This answer conceals two further dangers: first, that LEAs have already begun to misuse existing tests; second, the APU was accepted on the basis that the policy of 'light sampling' would be adhered to; this will count for little if LEAs use APU-type items for 'every child, every year' testing used as a crude (and completely unsatisfactory) method of identifying good and bad schools.

In July 1977 the Green Paper appeared. Brief references were made to the APU under the heading 'Standards and Assessment'. Paragraph 3.10 (p. 18) goes even further than the Selby document and appears to be encouraging LEAs to undertake blanket testing, although national blanket testing is rejected (para. 3.11).

3.10   The Departments are concerned with assessing individual pupils only as members of a representative sample, and this is the major function of the APU. A number of Educational Authorities have already decided on or are considering monitoring the performance of pupils in their areas: tests suitable for this purpose are likely to come out of the work of the APU. Here again the Department's concern is that there should be consistency within local education authorities and wherever possible between authorities.

3.11   It has been suggested that individual pupils should at certain ages take external 'tests of basic literacy and numeracy', the implication being that those tests should be of national character and universally applied. The Secretaries of State reject this view. Because of the differing abilities and rates of development of children of school age, tests pitched at a single level could be irrelevant for some and beyond the reach of others. Moreover the temptation for schools to coach for such tests would risk distorting the curriculum and possibly lowering rather than raising average standards.

Although a whole section of the Green Paper was devoted to 'special needs of minority groups' (p. 22-3) no mention of The APU is made in this context. Furthermore the 'major function' of the APU was defined in terms of national sampling rather than assisting particular groups.

During 1977 and 1978 five explanatory leaflets and two subject booklets (on Mathematics and Language) were produced by the DES/APU. None of them mention educational disadvantage. One of them (*APU: An Introduction*) gives a very different explanation from the White Paper on Educational Disadvantage:

> The last ten years have seen changes in school organisation and curriculum. We need to be able to monitor the consequences for children's performance in school. We need to know how our schools are serving the changing needs of children and society. That is why the Department of Education and Science set up the APU.

I would like to make clear at this stage that I would not wish to prejudge the value of the work of the APU. And I am not questioning that the HMI and others involved have the improvement of educational standards at heart. What I am suggesting is that the appearance of the APU on the education scene provides us with an interesting example of the DES 'using the back door' when they might have expected that their proposal would arouse anxieties and difficulties if more direct methods were used. Although the British civil service has often been praised for being non-political, in the party-political sense, civil servants are highly political in the sense of knowing how to get what they want; this particular diversionary tactic is fairly well known in politics:

> *Nigel Lawson*: 'Would you say it is easier for a Prime Minister in this country to do one thing if he says he is doing something else?'
> *Harold Macmillan*: 'It is a very common method, yes.'
> (Interview reported in *The Listener*, 8 September 1966,

quoted by A. Sampson, *Macmillan*, Allen Lane, 1967, p. 127)

The APU also provides us with an example of another trend: the DES extending a central influence over the curriculum. The reasons for this may be laudable: many would agree that LEAs and schools have neglected the study of the curriculum as a whole. But there is no guarantee that the DES influence (through the APU and in other ways) will be wholly beneficial. It was suggested in Chapter 3 that there are signs that the DES thinking has been too much influenced by American belief in management by behavioural objectives. And there is a serious danger that the APU could develop along exactly those lines. It would be fair to say that those in control of the APU at present and the recent past (Tom Marjoram and Brian Kay in particular) are aware of the excesses of American-style testing and evaluation. But they may be setting up machinery which could be used in ways that have been bitterly condemned by educationists in the USA (see, for example, Ernest House, 1974).

If at this moment I were asked to vote either to abolish the APU or to allow it to continue, I would want it to proceed with its activities. But there are political dangers which should be made known and discussed openly — the more openly the better.[2]

Influence on the curriculum

APU officers have been careful to say that they want to minimise the back-wash effect of monitoring. Any official test inevitably encourages 'teaching to the test' and the APU cannot avoid this however hard they try. It is, therefore, very important that the tests themselves should reflect good curriculum thinking rather than what is convenient to test. This will be particularly important when tests are developed for 'aesthetic' or 'personal and social' development, but it is already important even in much more easily tested subjects like Mathematics. What is tested one year will tend to become the curriculum for future years, so the choice, for example, between new and traditional mathematical items is very important.

There is also, unfortunately, an element of double-think on this issue about influencing the curriculum. On the one hand it is said that the tests will not influence the curriculum to any great extent; on the other hand, it is also said that aesthetic development should be tested (despite the enormous difficulties) because if it were not tested then the curriculum would be in danger of being unbalanced or impoverished.

It would be much better if it were openly acknowledged that monitoring will have an effect on the curriculum, maybe a considerable effect. It would then be possible to take those into account and plan accordingly.

The disclosure of results

APU publications emphasise the fact that when reports on performance are published it will not be possible to identify individual pupils, schools or LEAs. This is clearly the policy of the Unit at the time of writing (1979), and it is very important, for example, that schools in any area should not be set in some kind of league table according to test results. Such crude comparisons would of course be very misleading unless a good deal was also known about the catchment areas, IQ scores of pupils, etc. It must be stressed however that it would not be difficult for these results to become available either if there were a change of government or government policy, or if a combination of ingenuity and duplicity were used by a knowledgeable investigator.

A second danger has already been briefly referred to in this chapter: namely that APU testing may legitimise or even encourage very doubtful testing programmes conducted by LEAs. Diagnostic tests are sometimes already being used to establish or compare standards; out of date tests are used; a large number of LEAs are now planning 'blanket testing', that is testing all pupils in an age group. Where such testing programmes have been started, it is often difficult to resist demands of local politicians and others to publish the results, identifying schools in a very misleading kind of 'league table'. At a time of declining pupil numbers, such results can be misinterpreted and used even as a basis for school closures. This would be similar to the kind of American 'accountability' which has brought testing into disrepute in the USA.

Over-emphasis on national standards

It is recognised by a majority of educationists that assessment of pupils' performance is a very important (probably neglec-ted) aspect of education. But great care is needed in the development and use of tests: one of the dangers being that tests results expressed in clear arithmetic form may appear to be much more accurate and objective than they really are. Also it is necessary to distinguish between different kinds of tests. Testing can be of three kinds.

First, *criterion-referenced tests*, that is tests which are designed to find out whether a part of a taught syllabus has been successfully learned. Teachers often devise tests of this kind themselves, or they can be produced as part of a curriculum project package.

The second kind of test may be described as *diagnostic*, although its use is rather wider than the title might suggest. These are used to identify strengths and weaknesses of individual children in a specific area of the curriculum, for example, if a child is having difficulty in reading, a diagnostic test should pick out those skills in which he is deficient, so that the teacher can put them right. This category of tests would also include various kinds of individual aptitude tests.

The third category of tests is usually referred to as '*norm-referenced*'. These tests are designed to show how well a pupil (or a group of pupils) performs in relation to a much larger sample — usually a standardised norm. Thus a pupil (or a whole class) may appear to be average, or so much below or above the average for that age group. These norm-referenced tests can also be used, but probably less effectively, to show whether this year's age group is performing better or worse than a similar group five or ten years ago.

The APU will be developing tests of the third kind: that is norm-referenced tests essentially concerned with questions of standards. But many educationists would say that this kind of test ought to be at the bottom of the list of priorities rather than at the top. Such tests might help parents choose 'good' schools (if LEAs were foolish enough to publish them), and they would enable administrators to judge whether standards were going up or down (although there is some doubt about this); but they will not help teachers to test how effectively their pupils are performing on a specific syllabus, nor will such tests help them to diagnose individual abilities and weaknesses.[3]

In other words the APU is spending a vast amount of money (exactly how much is not known, but it is a very generous budget) on what ought to be a relatively low priority. Inevitably there is a danger that less money will be spent on the more essential and useful kinds of assessment.

Statistical problems

The APU monitoring programme relies on item-banking and the use of the Rasch model.[4] There are, however, a number of educational objections and technical difficulties associated with this kind of approach (see Goldstein and Blinkhorn, 1977, for details of this argument). In brief the kind of item-banking being used assumes that it is possible to identify test items as being of equivalent difficulty, and also that these groups of items can then be sorted into levels of difficulty. Both of these assumptions present practical and theoretical problems, but a third assumption is even more dubious. It is assumed by the Rasch model that the sequence or hierarchy of difficulties once established is the same for all children irrespective of what they have been taught or what methods have been used in their teaching.

There are several other problems, statistical and educational, which have to be faced. Some suggest that these problems are sufficiently great to make the work of the APU largely a wasted effort. So not only is a large amount of money being spent on what might be a low priority, but it may even turn out to be money spent on techniques which will not survive the test of time. If that happens then account-ability questions may be directed to the DES in relation to the legitimacy of the APU operation.

Conclusion

The APU has been chosen for particular scrutiny for three reasons. First as an example of DES secrecy – it is under-standable that they should seek to avoid conflict with teach-ers' unions and others, but the long-term consequences of this manoeuvre may be very serious. Second, as an example of the DES seeking to exert some controlling influence over certain aspects of the school curriculum. Finally as an example of a failure to plan effectively: the APU has been launched with far too little concern either for the technical problems involved, or for the unintended consequences of such an operation.

Summary

1   The APU is examined as an example of
    (i)   the DES proceeding by subterfuge rather than open discussion,
    (ii) the DES exerting some central influence on the curriculum.
2   The history of the APU is analysed, showing that what started (1974) as a means of monitoring the needs of the educationally disadvantaged, eventually became a national testing agency concerned with standards.
3   There are a number of serious dangers inevitably associated with the work of the APU:
    (i)   Backwash effects on the curriculum.
    (ii) The disclosure of results and misinterpretation of results.
    (iii) The over-emphasis on tests concerned with standards when there is a greater need for tests which will improve teaching and learning.

(iv) There are unsolved technical problems in using the particular model chosen for the APU.

Appendix The membership of the consultative committee

The chairman of the consultative committee was Professor Barry Supple. The other members are: Lord Alexander, Secretary, Association of Education Committees; K. A. Baird, acting higher education officer, National Association of Teachers in Further and Higher Education; Sister D. Bell, principal, Digby Stuart College, Roehampton; P. Boulter, director of education, Cumbria; P. J. Casey, education officer, Confederation of British Industry; A. Chalmers, dean of the School of Social Sciences, University of Sussex; J. Chalk, national president, National Association of Schoolmasters; R. E. Cave, senior education officer, Cambridgeshire; H. C. Cook, Sylvester County Junior School, Liverpool; P. Eley, National Council of Parent Teacher Associations; D. Fisher, education officer, Hertfordshire; G. Hainsworth, assistant education officer, Association of Municipal Authorities; K. S. Hopkins, assistant director of education, Mid Glamorgan; M. Hurst, joint chairman, Brook Street Bureau; A. Jarman, National Union of Teachers; K. Jones, parent and doctor; J. A. Lawton, Association of County Councils; Stuart Maclure, editor, *The Times Educational Supplement*.

J. Owen, chief education officer, Devon; Mrs M. Paterson, TUC; Mrs E. Price, educational researcher; E. D. G. Robinson, chairman, Salford Education Committee; Dr W. Roy, The Hewett School, Norwich; F. A. Smithies, chairman, NAS Education Committee; T. P. Snape, headmaster, King Edward VI School, Totnes; C. L. West, Middlecroft County Junior School, Chesterfield; D. H. Wilcockson, chief education officer, London Borough of Havering.

D. Wilkinson, headmaster, Wolganston Comprehensive School, Stafford; D. Winters, Hilton primary school, Newcastle upon Tyne; Miss S. D. Wood, joint hon. secretary, The Joint Four and secretary of the Association of Assistant Mistresses; Professor J. Wrigley, department of education, University of Reading; A. Yates, director, National Foundation for Educational Research.

Chapter 5

The Schools Council

The last thing I want to see is a Schools Council which is
the poodle of the Department. That is no way forward at
all. However, it is not unreasonable to suggest that there
should be wider representation of lay people and it is not
unreasonable to suggest that there should be wider discussions between my Department and the Schools Council
about some of the priorities for work. I have no desire to
change the Schools Council into a rubber stamp for
Ministers and officials at the Department.

(Mrs Shirley Williams in the House of
Commons on 17 February 1977[1])

In the years following 1964 the Schools Council emerged as
the most important body in England and Wales concerned
with the curriculum. Its influence in curriculum development
was considerable, yet it could never have been said to have
possessed control, or even much power, in curriculum matters.
Some see this as a missed opportunity to plan the curriculum
as a whole from a national point of view; others see it as a
blessed relief that the Schools Council was not allowed to
move in that direction. During the 1970s the Schools Council
was submitted to more and more criticism; its influence and
prestige declined; and some feared that it would be reduced
to becoming 'the poodle of the DES'. The reasons for these
developments and changes are politically very important and
have a good deal of relevance for future planning: in my view,

a strong Schools Council, properly constituted, will be required to play an important role in curriculum planning at all levels. That will be discussed in the final chapter; meanwhile it is important to survey the past and present roles of the Council.

I should perhaps declare an interest before beginning this review: I was a member of the Schools Council Programme Committee 1976-8, and also served on the Review Body (although I did not agree with all the proposals for reform).

The Schools Council for Curriculum and Examinations is an independent body. It was established by the Secretary of State for Education and Science in 1964 to undertake research and development work on the curriculum, and to advise the Secretary of State on matters of examination policy. The Schools Council is jointly financed by the DES and LEAs. It has funded over 160 curriculum research and development projects, and published a large number of reports, teachers' guides and packages of teaching materials resulting from curriculum projects.

The Schools Council has also commissioned research and development work in the field of public examinations, and it also is responsible for co-ordinating the activities of GCE and CSE examining boards. The political origins of the Schools Council have been well described by Maurice Kogan (1978) who was himself a Ministry of Education member of the short-lived Curriculum Study Group. The task of the Curriculum Study Group was to:

identify, analyse and publish accounts of curriculum development which might be of help and interest to the schools. Indeed most of their work, in the short period of time they were allowed to exist, consisted of preparing papers on methods of examining for the Secondary Schools Examinations Council. The Ministry soon disbanded the CSG because of a wave of anxiety from the teacher associations who thought that it was an attempt to take on the control of educational content. Nothing could be further from the truth, for it was essentially an attempt to enable the Ministry to inform others better as well as to clarify its own thinking about those aspects of the curriculum which should affect the larger policy decisions. There was internal struggle within the DES for some administrators wanted policy to be more closely affected by educational substance while others feared that no development would be safe for ever and the CSG should be located in a protected position away from the potential interference of reactionary Ministers or Permanent Secretaries. 'We shan't be here forever', remarked one of the more progressive senior administrators. Eventually, the DES joined with the Local Authority Associations and the teachers in creating the Schools Council for the Curriculum and Examinations. (Kogan, *The Politics of Curriculum Change*, 1978, pp. 63-4)

The Schools Council was set up on the recommendation of the Lockwood Committee (1964) which also recommended that the Schools Council should take over the duties of the Secondary Schools Examination Council from September 1964. There were still some fears in the teaching profession, and in particular in the teachers' unions, that an attempt was being made to gain greater central control of the curriculum; the Lockwood Report carefully pointed out that this was not the intention:

No-one is consciously seeking to erode the schools' responsibilities. Indeed, great strides have been made since the turn of the century in freeing the schools from detailed supervision of their work by local and central government: at both levels, the role of the inspectorate has become advisory rather than supervisory. (para. 12)

From the beginning it had been emphasised that the role of the Schools Council was not to determine schools' curricula, but to make available a wide choice of suggestions and materials:

In short our conclusions on the nature of the problem are as follows:
1 The present arrangements for determining the curriculum in schools and the related examinations are not working well; in particular, teachers have insufficient scope for making or recommending modifications in the curriculum and examinations.

69

2   Different arrangements are needed to achieve the balanced co-operation of the teachers, the Local Education Authorities, the Ministry of Education, the establishments of Higher and Further Education, and others, in the continuing process of modifying curriculum and examinations.
3   More resources and more effort should be devoted to co-operative study, research and development in this field. (Lockwood Report, para. 15)

A list of priorities was soon established by the Schools Council on a wider range of choices:

1   The primary schools curriculum
2   The curriculum for the early leaver
3   The sixth form
4   English teaching
5   Examinations for the 16-plus age group

In the years immediately following 1964, a good deal of interesting work on each of those five topics was undertaken, and many publications produced.

In May 1971 Geoffrey Caston, who had been one of the Joint Secretaries (from 1966 to 1970) wrote an article 'The Schools Council in Context' which almost eulogised the Council and its work during the 1960s.[2] He said that he wanted the Council to survive: 'Because I believe it embodies certain educational values which I think fundamental to the kind of vigorous and compassionate society of which I want to be a member. I will summarise these values in two concepts – pluralism and professionalism.' Caston's justification for the Council was essentially political and makes a very important contribution to the limited amount of serious literature on the Schools Council, in other words I agree with most of what he said. He uses the term pluralism to mean 'the dispersal of power in education'; this is a very useful concept applied both to the Schools Council and to the English educational system as a whole.

Education is an area of social activity in which the concentration of power can severely damage young people. They are, after all, compulsory inmates of the schools, and

thus, in a very real sense, their prisoners. This is so even
though the purpose of their imprisonment by society is
not punitive, but beneficent. It nevertheless involves the
exercise of power over them; it is forceful intervention in
their personal development. They can be harmed by the
misuse of this power so as to mould them in the image of
the state. Or, to put it in a less sinister way, by treating
them as instruments of some national manpower policy
rather than as self-determining individuals. That is the
obvious danger, but in Britain it would be more probable
that concentration of educational power would lead not so
much to its damaging misuse but to a disuse which could
be almost as bad. A centralised educational system can be
too timid to experiment, too careful of giving offence ever
to allow its professional adventurers a free hand. In such a
system, change, if it is to happen at all, has to happen
everywhere all at once. The consequences of failure are
then so awful that no-one ever dares to take the risk.
(*Journal of Curriculum Studies*, vol. III, no. 1, pp. 50-1)

By professionalism Caston means the exercise by individuals
of choice and judgment in the interests of their clients. Such
choices should be made in terms of a professional ethic.
Professionalism also includes the provision of this impartial
service in the light of relevant and up to date information. It
is on this basis that the professional denies any outside
authority the right to tell him how to do his job. Caston sees
the Schools Council as a means of fostering the development
of the curriculum. He did not underestimate the complexity
or difficulty of the task, but clearly believed that the Schools
Council was the right kind of organisation for it. He made
two more important points in the same article: it would be
important for the Schools Council to develop a kind of
professional authority, but not the kind of authority which
implies the right to enforce obedience; second (and this is
connected with the idea of living in a pluralist society), the
Schools Council should be more concerned to develop evidence rather than solutions on curricular matters.

These are very powerful arguments in favour of the Schools
Council and its policies. I have said that I almost entirely

71

agree with Caston's views. Why then did the Schools Council decline in prestige? Why during the 1970s has it been the victim of so much criticism?

Reasons for declining influence

The Schools Council has been criticised for a number of reasons, some more justified than others; some completely unfair.

1 By the end of the 1960s a certain amount of disenchantment with education was becoming evident. No longer was the money spent on education automatically accepted as highly desirable; in particular 'progressive education' came under attack in such publications as the first of the Black Papers (1969). Because the Schools Council was concerned with curriculum development it was automatically associated with progressive methods at a time when suggestions were increasingly made that what schools really needed was a return to traditional discipline and the three Rs.

2 This negative attitude to the work of the Schools Council later coincided with the financial crisis of the 1970s and cuts in educational expenditure. At a time when money had to be saved somewhere, the Schools Council looked an easy target (particularly to LEAs under pressure from finance committees to reduce expenditure). The question then began to be asked as to whether the Schools Council was giving value for money. When turned into a crude cost-benefit analysis, it could be shown that many projects had been very expensive but that the materials produced were being used by very few schools. In the early days it had been optimistically assumed by the Council that if a good project produced good materials then teachers would use them. (There is even an element of this kind of optimism in Geoffrey Caston's paper.) The problem of dissemination – spreading the good news – was badly neglected in the early years of the Council. So what educationists would regard as good project materials

simply did not reach teachers in schools: teachers often did not know about either the projects or their materials. A related problem was that some projects (particularly primary mathematics and science) were years ahead of the teachers' capabilities. *Science 5-13*, for example, is generally regarded as an excellent project with well-designed materials for pupils and teachers. But even when primary school teachers knew about the project they rarely used the materials – they simply lacked enough knowledge about science to use the materials with any confidence. The answer to this problem was obvious – in-service courses for teachers; but the Schools Council was not funded to do this. LEAs, who were responsible for in-service training, neglected this duty in a disgraceful way and then criticised the Schools Council for its failure.

3   The Schools Council became more and more identified with teachers' unions and teacher politicians. (The reasons for this will be discussed in 4 below.) The irony of this situation was that the strength of the teachers (or the teachers' unions) left the Schools Council open to attack; criticising the Council became the most effective way of weakening the position of teachers claiming to be the only group competent to discuss the curriculum. Throughout the 1970s there was much discussion of the role of governing bodies, for example, which often involved an attack on the teachers' claim to control the curriculum. The heretical suggestion was made that 'the curriculum is too important to be left to teachers' (Ann Corbett, 1976). The two slogans of 'accountability' and 'participation' when turned against the teaching profession generally, inevitably caused a reappraisal of the Schools Council, and particularly the doctrine of the teacher majority on all major committees.

4   The teacher majority question was, however, only one structural weakness in the unreformed Schools Council (i.e. up to 1978). A more serious weakness was the lack of full-time permanent appointments at the top of the Schools Council hierarchy. The Chairman was appointed, unpaid, for a limited period, and was expected to carry on with an existing full-time appointment elsewhere. If that

full-time appointment was something like directing a large polytechnic then the chairman could hardly be expected to provide leadership on a day-to-day basis. Moreover, the joint secretaries were also seconded for periods of about three years, so as committee members themselves grew more experienced the temporary joint secretaries tended to be at a considerable disadvantage. The result was that the largest and best organised group of committee members (from the NUT) began to dominate the Council, or at least some of it. This might have been avoided if the DES had been able to continue to second joint secretaries of the calibre of Derek Morrell and Geoffrey Caston, but it might also be argued that a structure which depends on the existence of such outstanding personalities is itself a poor one.

One of the most important of the 1978 changes was the replacement of three temporary joint secretaries by a permanent secretary as a career appointment. Other aspects of the constitutional review will be considered below.

5   Some of the proposals for examination reform made by the Schools Council (see Chapter 6) met with traditionalist opposition, including powerful elements within the DES. On this question of examinations a strange kind of rivalry developed between the DES and the Schools Council which can only be partly explained by the teacher majority situation referred to above. It was part of the Council's function to advise the Secretary of State on matters of examination policy. A clash between the DES and the Council on the question of 'A' level examination gradings occurred and an even more important dispute about the common examination at 16-plus.

The important question of examination policy at 16-plus reached a climax in 1976. Having generated a considerable amount of work on feasibility studies and other aspects of the examination, the Council made a strong recommendation to the Secretary of State that GCE 'O' level and CSE should be combined into a single examination system. It was, of course, the Secretary of State's responsibility to make a final decision. Presumably not an individual, personal decision but based on the advice of DES civil servants who by definition were amateurs on such questions. When the Secretary of State did not immediately accept the proposals made by the professional Schools Council but appeared to pay more attention to the amateur advice of civil servants, it was a difficult conflict situation for the DES to appear to be in. On such occasions it might be suspected that the DES would have preferred a weaker or more compliant Schools Council – hence the 'poodle' quotation which begins this chapter. It would have been more convenient for the DES to have had an apparently 'professional' body which gave it exactly the advice it wanted rather than advice which conflicted with its own views. It remains to be seen whether this will be a feature of the reformed Schools Council, but during 1976 at least one attempt was made by the DES to discredit the Schools Council in the eyes of the Secretary of State and the Prime Minister. This occurred in a section of the 'secret' Yellow Book which infuriated Council members at the time and caused the chairman, Sir Alex Smith, to demand an interview with the Secretary of State:

> Schools Council 48.   In the early 60s it became apparent to the Department that a positive initiative was required to promote innovation in the school curriculum. This led to the setting up within the Department of a Curriculum Study Group with the objectives described in its Annual Report for 1962.

> 49   However, despite the care which the group took to emphasise its respect for the responsibilities of teachers and LEAs, opposition to it led the then Minister to decide that the work of the CSG as well as that of the Secondary School Examinations Council (a body with a relatively long history) should be absorbed into an independent body called the Schools Council, which was set up in 1964, with the following terms of reference:
> 'The object of the Schools Council shall be the promotion of education by carrying out research into and keeping under review the curricula, teaching methods and examinations in schools, including the organisation of schools so far as it affects their curricula'.

50   The Schools Council has performed moderately in commissioning development work in particular curricular areas; has had little success in tackling examination problems, despite the availability of resources which its predecessor (the SSEC) never had; and it had scarcely begun to tackle the problems of the curriculum as a whole. Despite some good quality staff work the overall performance of the Schools Council has in fact, both on curriculum and on examinations, been generally mediocre. Because of this and because the influence of the teachers' unions has led to an increasingly political flavour – in the worst sense of the word – in its deliberations, the general reputation of the Schools Council has suffered a considerable decline over the last few years. In the light of this recent experience it is open to question whether the constitution of the Schools Council strikes the right balance of responsibility for the matters with which it deals. These issues could come to a head later this year in the context of the Council's recommendations to the Secretary of State about examinations.

51   Nevertheless, the Schools Council has carried out and published a considerable volume of work in the field of the curriculum and examinations, and some of the development projects which it has commissioned have made a valuable contribution to the development of the schools curriculum. (DES, Yellow Book)

A nice piece of political drafting, designed to spike the guns of the Schools Council on the particular issue of the 16-plus common examination, and to discredit the work of the Council generally. It has been suggested – but there is no proof of this – that this was not simply the work of the DES but the fruit of an alliance between the DES officials and HMI who also resented the Council. This however must remain a speculation until the documents are eventually made available. At a time when education generally was under attack it must, however, have been very convenient for HMI and DES to have had such an easy scapegoat so readily available.

An evaluation of the Schools Council's achievements

In view of the Yellow Book's criticisms, I would like to put forward a more objective evaluation of the Council's record:

1 Development work

To describe the Schools Council performance in this field as 'moderate' is very unfair. The number of projects (over 160) was impressive, as was the general quality of the work. Of course there have been failures and disappointments, but there have also been outstanding successes. For example, the Humanities Curriculum Project has not only produced excellent packs of materials for use in schools with a very difficult age group (the 14-16-year-olds) but has also generated a whole series of research projects designed to make practising teachers more actively involved in the processes of curriculum change and evaluation; a number of schools have been transformed and hundreds of teachers revitalised by this project. Although some aspects of the work are controversial, the project has been regarded with admiration by curriculum experts in a number of overseas countries.

It is equally true that much of the work in the main curriculum subjects — mathematics, science, history and geography — has been of extremely high quality.

The major weakness has been in dissemination. The Schools Council has not solved this problem, but neither has anyone else in any other country! The Schools Council was slow in realising that there was a major problem here, but the Council had already begun tackling this difficult area long before the Review in 1976-8.

2 Examination problems

There are two main problems: reform of the examination system at 16-plus and 18-plus; comparability of standards between Boards.

Common examination at 16-plus

It has been quite clear for a number of years that the practice of dividing secondary-school pupils into GCE and CSE 'types' was an undesirable perpetuation of the discredited Spens and Norwood view that children could be neatly separated into water-tight categories of that kind. A single examination at 16-plus was urgently needed as a means of enabling comprehensive schools to become much more comprehensive and to develop common curricula whilst maintaining standards of excellence. The Schools Council in 1976 declared that such an examination (or, more correctly, *system* of examinations) was not only desirable but feasible. The DES had doubts – partly financial, partly based on obsolete elitist views of curriculum and examinations. They advised the Secretary of State not to reject the Schools Council proposal but to delay a verdict and to carry out further investigations (despite the fact that a considerable number of feasibility studies had already been undertaken). This was, of course, one of the issues which the Yellow Book expected to 'come to a head later this year'. The Secretary of State therefore did not accept the Schools Council recommendation but instead set up the Waddell Committee which in 1978 came to exactly the same conclusions as the Schools Council at a cost of £195,909. It might also be assumed that part of the DES thinking was in terms of a change of government between 1976 and 1978 which might well have caused the Schools Council's proposals to be completely vetoed.

GCE reforms at 'A' level

It has long been recognised that the sixth-form curriculum is far too specialised. Many attempts have been made to avoid over-specialisation, some of them before the Schools Council existed (e.g. the Agreement to Broaden the Curriculum in 1961) but none have succeeded. The Schools Council's committees have done a good deal of work in this area but so far have failed to produce a formula which would satisfy everyone (the universities in particular). It is difficult to see how a two-year curriculum can be 'broadened' without some loss either in depth or on content coverage. If universities wish to insist on the continuation of 'A' level syllabuses as a prerequisite for university entrance then there simply is no solution to this problem, and it is a little hard to put the blame on the Schools Council. A compromise of some kind is necessary, and it may be that the price universities will eventually demand for such a compromise will be a four-year degree course. Meanwhile the Schools Council was subject to a variety of criticisms for its Q and F proposals (1969) which appeared to be unacceptable to the users, and the N and F proposals in 1978-9 ran into exactly the same kind of difficulties (see Chapter 6).

Comparisons of standards between examining boards

It is one of the functions of the Schools Council to make sure that CSE, GCE 'O' and 'A' level standards are rougly equivalent between the various boards operating these examinations. It is also their responsibility to achieve comparability between CSE Grade 1 and passes at 'O' level. Many experts doubt whether this exercise can be carried out with any high degree of accuracy or meaningfulness, but in so far as it is possible the Schools Council's record in this area is exemplary.[3]

3 The whole curriculum

It is true that the Council's work on the whole curriculum (especially the Working Papers on the Middle School Curriculum and the Secondary School Curriculum) has not been of the highest quality. It might also be said that HMI, free of committee restraints, had not produced anything of note by 1976 either. Since the Yellow Book has been published, however, 'Curriculum 11-16' has appeared, and although I personally welcome its publication, it is probably true to say that its overall quality is too patchy to meet the standards required of Schools Council publications.

4 The 'political flavour' of the Schools Council

This accusation is not entirely without foundation, but its

importance has been exaggerated. Most committees rarely vote on issues, and it is by no means always possible to 'place' a committee member from the points he chooses to make. It is probably true that the NUT (and others) have much to learn from the DES about how to be highly political and still retain a reputation for being completely non-political. Sir Alex Smith, the Chairman from 1975 to 1978, summed it up when he said he trusted the Secretary of State and he trusted the teachers, but he did not trust the DES. Teachers' Unions have, however, been too insistent on the doctrine of teacher autonomy – in the over-simplified form of asserting that only teachers have a right to make decisions about the curriculum.

The review of the Schools Council constitution (1977-8)

A review of some kind was clearly needed, but it remains to be seen whether the revised constitution will be the right one. The replacement of three temporary joint secretaries by permanent officers will be a considerable advantage. In addition the abolition of governing council and its replacement by a convocation (on which teachers will be in a minority) will be an improvement and will result in a wide range of constituencies being represented. The streamlining of committees, with the Programme Committee being abolished and to some extent being replaced by a Professional Committee (which retains its teacher majority) should also work reasonably well. There was, however, a more fundamental revision: whereas the pre-1978 structure (figure 5.1) was essentially vertical and hierarchical; the revised structure (figure 5.2) is horizontal, with three major committees of theoretically equivalent status. When a pronouncement is made from 'the Schools Council' it will be on the basis of consensus between the three committees. In some respects this will be a great advantage, not least in eliminating the final power resting with the single committee – Governing Council – and the almost inevitable block voting at that stage. But there is also one serious political danger inherent in the structure: all matters involving policy priorities and the allocation of money will have to have the approval of the Finance and Priorities

Committee, the composition of which is roughly one-third teachers, one-third DES and one-third LEA. The danger is that those who are increasingly referred to as the 'paymasters' (DES and LEA) have an automatic two-thirds majority. They will not always agree, but when they do any forward-looking proposal from the Professional Committee may be blocked. During 1978 certain fears were expressed that at a time when the LEAs were almost entirely Conservative in their representation, a change of government would give the Finance and Priorities Committee a very powerful veto on any proposals which appear to be innovatory in any radical sense.

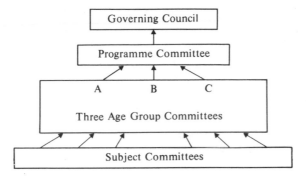

Figure 5.1 Simplified model of Schools Council committee structure: pre-1978 (vertical)

Figure 5.2 Simplified model of Schools Council committee structure: post-1978 (horizontal)

During the deliberations of the Review Body, there were clear misgivings about this possibility of professional proposals in effect being vetoed for reasons which might be only ostensibly financial. But the Review Body was meeting at a time when there was still a threat that the Schools Council might be completely abolished by the Secretary of State.

When the composition of the Finance and Priorities Committee was being discussed, the teachers on the Review Body had clearly received the message that if they did not agree to the Finance and Priorities Committee being firmly in the control of the paymasters, then there might be no Schools Council at all. As an additional incentive the teachers were promised and given a clear majority on the Professional Committee. A more charitable view would be that the DES and LEAs argued that if they were to continue supporting the Schools Council financially then they must be more deeply involved in its work and management. A by-product of that should be that LEAs will become much more involved in the implementation and dissemination than they have been in the past.

Despite this it is to be hoped that the constitution of the new Schools Council will work well in practice. A strong Schools Council or something like it is essential for the reasons given by Geoffrey Caston. Whether it works in the long run will depend on political factors – in both senses of the word.

Summary

1   The Schools Council arose (1974) out of the ashes of the Curriculum Study Group. The abandonment of the Curriculum Study Group as a result of an alliance between teachers and LEAs might be seen as a partial victory over the DES.
2   Teachers were given a majority on all important Schools Council Committees.
3   In the late 1960s and early 1970s the Schools Council was criticised for two reasons: (a) for being too 'progressive', (b) for being teacher-dominated.
4   The Yellow Book (1976) was unfairly critical of the Schools Council's past performance.
5   DES opposed Schools Council recommendations for examination reforms 1978.
6   The review of the Schools Council constitution was completed in 1978, involving a loss of power for teachers, and putting financial control firmly in the hands of DES and LEA representatives.

Chapter 6

The control of the examination system

Introduction

If it is true that a major constraint on secondary education is the external examination system, then its control is of crucial political significance. It is often said that secondary teachers are, in theory, free to devise their own curricula, but in practice an important set of limitations is imposed by the system of public examinations at 16-plus and 18-plus which are so important in England. Of all the constraints on secondary teachers' freedom – HMI, local advisers, governors, parents and employers – the examination system is most frequently mentioned and complained about. For many secondary teachers, the examination provides not only a means of assessment but a set of objectives as well. Many teachers asked about their objectives would simply reply 'to get as many pupils as possible successfully through the examinations'. Teachers, who are apparently proud of their freedom, have accepted a system which includes syllabuses written by a board external to the school, examinations set and marked by externals, and with little or no account taken of teachers' judgments in the final assessment of pupils. How did such a system originate? Why has it been accepted for so long? What changes are taking place? What are the chances of teachers gaining more control over the system? These are the main questions which need to be answered in this chapter.

Unfortunately, there is still a good deal of detailed research to be done in this area and conclusive answers will not always be possible. Petch (1953) has written an account of fifty years history of one board[1] which throws a good deal of light on general questions of control; Pearce (1972) has produced a more polemical account of examinations, and was particularly concerned about the inadequate representation of classroom teachers on the various examining boards; Montgomery (1965) has written an excellent history of examinations to which I am greatly indebted. But many of the detailed questions remain unanswered: for example, information about Secretaries to the Boards, Chief Examiners and Moderators. Not only factual information about their social and professional background but their educational views and ideological positions. All that must wait upon many more detailed studies.

It may be important to begin by stressing that it would be extremely simple-minded to assume that examinations are an evil (even a necessary evil). There have been times – as we shall see in the account of nineteenth-century developments – when examinations were generally on the side of the angels. During the twentieth century, however, it has become more and more common to criticise examinations for restricting desirable curriculum change; this was one of the major themes of the Norwood Report (1943), and has been an important issue in secondary education ever since. But evaluation and assessment of some kind are essential in education, and it is not always clear whether the examination debate is about the efficiency of examinations as a form of assessment, or the control of the examinations by non-teachers or teachers who are unrepresentative.

There is another argument which lies behind some of the following account of the development of examination structures. Teachers must be accountable in some way to local and central authorities; if they resist any attempts, whether local or central, to influence the *content* of the curriculum then this serves to strengthen the position of those who demand that the evaluation (in the form of terminal examinations) must not be in the hands of the teachers themselves, but that independent, 'public' examining is essential. This will be one of the features of the debate about CSE Mode III examinations and the question of the common examination at 16-plus.

One further distinction needs to be made by way of introduction. Assessment can usefully be divided into two (overlapping) categories: criterion-referenced and norm-referenced tests or forms of assessment. Criterion-referenced tests should be used when an individual candidate is required to demonstrate his mastery over a specific set of skills or minimum amount of knowledge. The driving test is a good example of a criterion-referenced test. The candidate has to demonstrate such pre-specified skills as steering, use of brakes, signals, etc., as well as 'knowledge' of the Highway Code. He must pass on every item — competence is required on all the criteria specified. A norm-referenced test, however, is designed to show where a candidate should be placed in relation to other candidates. One norm is the average score for all candidates, and a candidate can be said to be above or below average, or more sophisticated measures of superiority and inferiority can be used, usually in terms of percentage scores.

Both types of test can involve pass and failure, but the concepts will be different in each case. With the driving test there is no attempt to assess (or predict) whether a candidate is (or will become) above average; he simply passes the test by demonstrating his proficiency across the range of items. In the GCE examination, however, each candidate is graded according to certain 'norms' and one of the norms (maybe a mark of 45 out of 100) is the score above which candidates will pass and below which they will fail.[2] Those with scores above the pass mark may then be graded in bands which might be labelled A, B, C.

One of the differences between the two types of assessment is that norm-referenced testing is intrinsically competitive: the success of one candidate depends not just on his own performance, but on how well or badly other candidates perform. It would, of course, be possible to have norm-referenced tests without involving the idea of failure (and that was the original intention of the CSE). Without 'failure' the main intention would be to give a profile of scores across a range of subjects to illustrate the relative strengths and weaknesses of each candidate.

Further details of GCE and CSE examinations will be given later, but it will be worth noting that there is a very strong connection in England between norm-referenced tests and the idea of *selection*. Hence the criticism that not only is the curriculum distorted by the examination system, but that this distortion encourages the classification of pupils into 'successes and failures', 'academic and non-academic', or 'university material and non-starters'. Furthermore, it has encouraged schools to spend an inordinate amount of their resources on the minority of university-bound pupils at the expense of the vast majority of children. English secondary-school examinations strongly reflect a competitive and divisive 'keeping-out' mentality rather than a general 'enlightening' policy in education. The roots of the tendency are to be found in the nineteenth-century development of secondary-school examinations.

The nineteenth-century background: from patronage to competition

By about the middle of the nineteenth century patronage in private and public employment was beginning to be condemned as corrupt and inefficient. The utilitarian philosophy prevalent at that time advocated efficiency in the conduct of government, including the army and the civil service, and one suggested reform was selection by written examinations as a test of fitness for public positions.

We have seen in Chapter 2 that another result of this drive for efficiency was the Committee of the Privy Council's decision (1839) to superintend the grants given to schools, by *inspection*, to ensure efficient expenditure of government money. In the 1840s HMI used written examinations as a means of selecting and qualifying elementary-school teachers. The establishment of new departments, and the growing tendency of the government to be involved in police, railways, health, merchant shipping and joint stock companies, led to a need for more bureaucratic and efficient transaction of public business. The old method of selecting civil servants through a system of patronage made it difficult to carry out all these new government responsibilities with the efficiency that was thought desirable.

86

In 1853 the Indian civil service had taken the lead by making entry to the service subject to *competitive* examinations. A Committee of Enquiry into the organisation of the home civil service was set up in the same year, headed by Stafford Northcote and C. P. Trevelyan. They recommended far-reaching reforms. The Civil Service Commission was established in the following year, but competitive examinations for the entire home civil service did not begin until 1870.

It is interesting to note that a little earlier a similar move had been taking place within the universities. Oxford University had introduced examination reform as early as 1800 with the appointment of examiners and the award of honours degrees based on written examinations. Cambridge followed soon afterwards, and a Royal Commission investigating the state of Oxford University in 1852 accepted examinations as an inevitable part of the university system.

The success of university examinations encouraged university teachers to demand evidence that undergraduates had reached a suitable standard *before* arrival at the university; in other words, that similar examinations ought to be introduced into the schools. By this time schools, public and endowed, were already involved in examinations. Some of them were training boys for the Indian Civil Service Entrance Examination, as well as entry to the Army by the qualifying test which had been introduced in 1849. Manchester Grammar School set up a special Civil Service Form in 1869 in anticipation of the competitive examinations for the home civil service. These examinations were not welcomed by all schoolmasters, but the trend in the direction of competitive examinations was firmly established. An additional incentive to develop school examinations was that patronage was gradually being replaced by examinations as a means of entry into many of the professions.

An important landmark was the establishment of Oxford and Cambridge 'Locals' in 1858. The Oxford Locals involved both examination and inspection of schools: there were separate regulations for examination and inspection but it was not easy to distinguish between them. (Inspection of secondary schools by HMIs was not possible until the Board of Education was created at the beginning of the twentieth century.) The origin of the 'Locals' was that some 'middle-class' schools had adopted the practice of commissioning an independent evaluation of the school from a respected outsider, such as a local clergyman or a fellow of an Oxford or Cambridge College. This was, however, an expensive practice, and the majority of schools – particularly those most in need of inspection – did not have any external report. It was therefore very difficult to compare standards of schools or to judge their efficiency. In 1857 the Bath and West of England Society for the Encouragement of Agriculture, Arts, Manufacture and Commerce set up a committee to organise an examination for local schoolboys (the 'Exeter Experiment'). T. D. Acland, with a double first from Oxford, was one of the organisers, and he ensured the involvement of the universities. Temple, another successful Oxford man (later Archbishop of Canterbury) was also involved. The examination was competitive, and a list of honours published.

It was not intended that this should be an annual event, but it was hoped that the examination would be taken over by a more powerful body, and the universities were an obvious choice. Cambridge as well as Oxford responded to the challenge: both sets of 'Locals' began in 1858. Some years later the custom of issuing certificates began in Oxford (1877). The age of school examinations controlled by university boards had begun. A later development, but one which was ultimately to be even more influential, was the University of London Matriculation Examination. London Matriculation regulations had existed since 1839 when nine subjects were demanded; by 1908 the number of subjects had been reduced to five, and the examination had become established as a means of indicating academic achievement for many who did not intend entering university. (By this time there was also a lower level Junior School Leaving Certificate (1903) and a Higher School Leaving Certificate (1905) for older pupils.) Other universities adopted similar procedures, partly to satisfy the needs of the schools (school leaving examinations), and partly to set standards for university entrance (matriculation examinations). By the end of the nineteenth century the situation was still patchy and completely lacking in uniformity.

The growth and development of examinations to the establishment of Secondary Schools Examinations Council (1917)

The end of the nineteenth century and the beginning of the twentieth century was a period of considerable growth in public examinations. Some examinations which began as a means of assessing the standards of individual pupils, increasingly became a useful means of judging the qualities of schools. It was possible for examinations to meet both requirements so long as there was public confidence in those running the examinations. Because there was much more confidence in the high status universities than in most middle-class schools, universities gradually increased their participation in and control over examinations. In 1903 the northern universities formed their own Joint Matriculation Board (JMB) with an examination planned along similar lines to the London matriculation. This examination was also used for much wider purposes than university entrance. Throughout the period various professional bodies were encouraged to use matriculation examinations rather than devise their own: this was probably a result of the fairly well-accepted view that although examinations were splendid educational devices, too many of them would be harmful and counter-productive.

For this reason and because there was a need for greater uniformity, various suggestions were made to establish a central council for school examinations. The advantages of this were obvious, but there were widespread fears about centralisation as well. It was still regarded, not merely by teachers, as a grave danger to have central control of examinations in the hands of a state department. But there was as yet insufficient confidence in the teachers to allow them to run a national system of examinations themselves: the College of Preceptors in 1903 failed to get their examinations recognised by the Board of Education, and this probably reflected a general view that examinations should be run by a group of experts independent of the schools and the teachers, although teachers became increasingly involved in the marking of examination papers (suitably supervised by university examiners).

Gradually all non-university examining bodies were

squeezed out, so that by 1917 control of the school examinations was firmly in the hands of the universities: the only alternative seemed to be state control in the form of the Board of Education. The Secretary of the Board, Lingen, in 1858 had wisely avoided that political route and refused to allow the Education Committee to take over the Exeter experiment. The Taunton Report (1868) had also recommended a central council for examinations but this was not acted upon. The Bryce Report (1895) recommended a central office for examinations, but after the Acts of 1899 and 1902 the newly created local education authorities preferred to recognise the universities rather than give increasing power to the central authority.

By the beginning of the twentieth century the Board was less reluctant to get involved in policy-making about examinations: for example, in 1904 the Board interfered by forbidding external examinations in the first two years at secondary schools; but the Board still did not make a bid for outright control, preferring to exercise as much control as possible indirectly.

In 1917, after extensive consultations between the Board, universities and professional bodies, a compromise formula was found in the shape of a 'balanced' Secondary Schools Examinations Council (SSEC) which would advise the Board.[3] The Council consisted of twenty-one members: five LEA representatives, six representing the teachers, and ten representing the university examining bodies. Its first task was to co-ordinate the new School Certificate and Higher Certificate examinations (set by the separate university examining bodies), and to maintain standards which would be respected nationally. This made their second task much easier – discouraging other bodies from setting up new examinations at 16-plus and 18-plus.

Over the years the 'balance' of SSEC representation changed, and this is usually a good indicator of change in influence. For example, in 1936 membership was increased to 30 – 10 from each of the three groups, thus effectively reducing university influence; in 1946 the Minister of Education, wanting more central control, removed *all* the representatives from university examining bodies.[4] Control of the examinations was evidently seen as much more important than central control of curricula. Nevertheless a good deal of power remained with the Boards who set and marked the examinations. One of the enduring complaints about public examinations (for example, in the Spens Report, 1938) was that they were dominated by the universities, and that the school curriculum was sacrificed to university entrance requirements.

From School Certificate to GCE

During the inter-war years the number of pupils taking school-certificate examinations increased rapidly, but the structure was often criticised. The main reason for the unpopularity of the School Certificate was that it was a group examination. The teaching profession — especially secondary-school head-mistresses and assistant teachers — found it frustrating that a number of pupils every year achieved good overall results but did not reach the prescribed standard in a modern language or in mathematics or science (about 30 per cent of those failing were in this category).

The School Certificate was a group examination in two senses: a certificate was only granted if a candidate passed in five subjects; and these five subjects had to cover certain groups. In 1917 there were three main subject groups: (1) English subjects, (2) foreign languages (classical or modern), (3) science and mathematics. A candidate, in order to gain a certificate, had to satisfy the examiners in five subjects, including one subject from each of these groups. Part of the 'theory' behind this was the ideal of 'general education', but there was also a continuing need to make secondary education quite distinctive from the curriculum of elementary schools and later on from the central, commercial and technical schools. Group 4 subjects (art, music and practical subjects) were regarded as inferior, and candidates could only offer one subject from this group. This structure was gradually relaxed in two ways: by increasing the range of subjects in Group 4 and by allowing candidates to choose more than one subject from that group. In 1937 a joint committee of the four secondary associations recommended that the group system be abolished and that candidates should be given a certificate on the basis of *any* five subjects, *plus* a compulsory test in English. This was, however, opposed by sections of the teaching profession, especially the NUT (see Banks, 1955, p. 91). In the following year, 1938, the Secondary Schools Examination Council accepted a compromise proposal: namely that candidates be allowed a choice between groups (2) and (3) – that is, that proficiency was demanded in either a modern language or in mathematics and science, but no longer in both. In effect, the only compulsory subject was English language.

Thus the hardship of one aspect of the group system was alleviated. But another problem remained: the connection between the School Certificate examination and 'matriculation'. As we have seen, matriculation was originally designed as a test of minimum entrance qualification to a university degree. It was felt that before specialising on a narrow degree course, candidates should display evidence of 'general education': hence the requirement of five subjects to be passed at *credit* standard in School Certificate, including English, mathematics or science, and a foreign language. From 1917 until 1951 (but especially at times of high unemployment) prospective employers tended to demand the superior 'matriculation' rather than the School Certificate as a desirable school leaving qualification. This undoubtedly increased the desire of many secondary-school teachers and head teachers to replace the School Certificate and matriculation structure by a system which was less restrictive and less demanding. Olive Banks (1955) suggests that the most persistent pressure group in this respect was the Association of Headmistresses whose pupils were often penalised by the requirement of a pass in either mathematics and in science.

The Norwood Report and after

The major official influence on 'reforming' the School Certificate was the Norwood Report (1943). The way this came about is not without political interest. The 1937 Investigators'

Report recommended that the SSEC should appoint a committee to initiate a long-term policy involving fundamental changes in school examinations. The recommendation was accepted by the Board of Education and the announcement made by the President of the Board of Education, H. Ramsbottom, on 2 January 1941. According to Petch (1953) the nomination of members was left entirely to the Chairman, Sir Cyril Norwood, formerly headmaster of Harrow School.

> From the outset he showed that he held strong opinions as to what should be its final recommendations. He was unable to carry his Committee all the way with him and this may to some extent explain the vague generalising in the report, its frequent woolly tendentiousness and the readiness to shuffle on to other shoulders the need to reach a final conclusion.

Petch also comments on the unusual procedures followed afterwards:

> The circumstances in which the Norwood Report was published could serve as a perfect example of that departmental procedure which to the uninitiated seems like official chicanery. It might have been expected that, since the Norwood Committee had originated as a Committee of the SSEC, it would report in the first instance to the Council. Instead the report went to Mr. R. A. Butler, who in July 1941 had succeeded Mr. Ramsbottom, and it was published in June 1943 without reference to the Council. In the following November the Council was summoned to a two day meeting, the only substantial item of business being the Norwood Report. On assembly the members were bluntly informed that their part was to receive and not to question; when it began to appear that considerable comment was likely, the Chairman unceremoniously dismissed them after only two hours. The Council was not summoned again until Miss Ellen Wilkinson had carried out her purge; the meeting in November 1943 was the last occasion on which the examining bodies took part in the proceedings of the SSEC. (Petch, 1953, p. 164-5)

We should bear in mind the partiality of this evidence – Petch, the Secretary of one of the examining boards, felt very strongly about the exclusion of the examining bodies at this crucial stage in the history of examinations.

From the beginning of the twentieth century the balance of the curriculum had been achieved by control from outside schools: external examinations in the hands of 'independent' university examining boards. This was changed by the post-Norwood arrangements. Why this took place is an interesting question, but it is not clear whether the answer lies in the Norwood Report itself or in the events surrounding the Report.

The Norwood Report recommendations

This is a document which was much criticised at the time and more recently, but it was nevertheless extremely influential in determining post-war educational policies. In some respects it was essentially backward-looking: in the first chapter the discredited psychology of the 1930s was accepted in a totally uncritical way. It was accepted that there were three types of pupil who needed three different kinds of curriculum – the grammar, the technical and the modern. The three types of pupil, it was assumed, would be best catered for in three separate schools. Most pupils would go to secondary modern schools at age eleven and be free from the restriction of any examinations.

It is very important to look at the examination recommendations of the Norwood Report, bearing in mind that when the report talks of teachers having more responsibility and control, only the elite of the profession were to be involved. It is quite clear that the idea of handing over control of examinations to secondary modern teachers (mainly ex-elementary teachers) was not part of the Norwood plan.

In the case of grammar and public schools, however, Norwood criticised the School Certificate examinations for dominating and distorting the curriculum. In future it was suggested that examinations should play only a subordinate role and should also 'ideally' be conducted by the teachers themselves. This would take time, but was the eventual goal.

The three most important recommendations about the 16-plus examination were as follows:

1   The School Certificate should continue to be run by university examining bodies — there should be a standing committee of eight teachers, four LEA representatives, and four university representatives, *supported by four HMI as assessors.*
2   Schools should offer their own syllabuses (and some of the prescribed syllabuses should be lightened).
3   Examinations should be subject examinations, that is, without restriction as to numbers of subjects or groups.

It was also recommended that there should be much more emphasis placed on school records: there was a need for teachers to improve their judgment and rely less on external examination.

The third recommendation was the most important, historically and politically. In retrospect it might be suggested that such freedom for the schools could only work if there were some other external means of supervising or controlling the curriculum. The Norwood solution to this problem (never explicitly stated, but perhaps considered) was a much larger force of HMIs. HM Inspectorate, it was suggested, had survived their unfortunate early history associated with payment by results and a narrow view of inspection, and should now be regarded as advisers. Full inspections should take place every five years, supplemented by informal visits. 'The Norwood Committee was extravagant in its commendation of HM Inspectorate and urged yet greater extension' (Petch, p. 164).

Another criticism of the Norwood Report was that the substitution of school reports for external examinations would place a very heavy burden on head teachers, and give considerable advantage to pupils from well known schools. Such criticisms were, however, ignored by the Labour government's Minister of Education, Ellen Wilkinson, who supported the abolition of the old School Certificate. Before the SSEC had given advice on the Norwood proposals Ellen Wilkinson (an ex-teacher) changed the constitution of the Council. Circular 113 (June 1946) made the Minister *fully* responsible for co-ordinating secondary school examinations: examining boards would co-operate but were not to be involved in decision-making.

In August 1947 the new SSEC made its first report.

> To the general surprise the report was unanimous. It was common knowledge that the new Council included an element in favour of abolition of public examinations for grammar school and that some members were hypnotised by the claims for objective tests. There were the egalitarians for whom the provision of 'secondary education for all' meant that the grammar schools must not be allowed the advantages which might arise if their pupils could sit for certificates not available to the secondary modern and the secondary technical schools. There were also those who were ready to abolish the existing examining bodies and to substitute either the Ministry itself or the new central examining body under the control of officialdom. That so many heterogeneous elements ultimately reached unanimity can only be a matter for wonderment, and for conjecture as to how it was done. (Petch, p. 167)

It is interesting that most of the controversy about the new structure concerned the age limit rather than the major departure from the traditional group certificate. The 1947 report did not allow pupils to take GCE before the age of sixteen, and this was removed, after much protesting from head teachers, in 1952, on the grounds that it had been intended that intelligent pupils could by-pass the 'O' level examination and move straight on to their 'A' level work.

Another move in the direction of exclusiveness rather than expansion in secondary education was that the new pass level at GCE 'O' level was considerably higher than a pass at School Certificate (it was intended to be roughly equivalent to the old credit grade). The reasons for making that decision, apart from the ever-acceptable claim of raising standards, remain unclear. If the intention was to abolish school examinations for all but a small minority, then that policy was clearly doomed to failure: examinations were too well entrenched as the system.

The influence of the universities over the 16-plus examination was reduced by the removal of examining bodies from

SSEC; they were however in a much stronger position when it came to university entrance qualifications. In 1949 the Committee of Vice Chancellors and Principals called a conference which rejected the idea of relying on school reports rather than examinations, and also defined carefully new matriculation requirements. Five GCE passes were to be required, at least two at 'A' level. The passes had to include English, another language, and a pass in either mathematics or a science subject. The hostility between the Ministry and the universities was illustrated by the fact that no prior consultation took place with schools or with the Ministry, either on the minimum entry requirements or on 'faculty requirements' which were more detailed and somewhat more demanding. Universities indicated that they wished to retain the idea of 'general education' despite the absence of a group certificate; unfortunately the shortage of university places eventually led schools to concentrate on a narrow range of work in the sixth form (getting good grades in two or three 'A' levels became essential for admittance to a university) and this tended to work against the idea of a good general education.

The distribution of power over the examination structure changed significantly in the post-war years. The Minister, Ellen Wilkinson, clearly wanted more central control of examinations; her successor, George Tomlinson, continued this policy, despite his professed ignorance about the curriculum (examinations and curriculum seemed to be regarded more separately at that time, despite the Norwood Report). An enhanced role for HM Inspectorate was recommended by Norwood, but this had little direct effect on the control of examinations: if the idea of school records and school-based examinations had been adopted then the power of the Inspectorate would almost certainly have increased dramatically. Montgomery (1965) sees the constitution of SSEC as a crucial factor in the distribution of power (in his chapters 3 and 6). The removal of representatives of examining bodies from the SSEC was one important change; the increase in the Ministry's nominees from six to eight members in 1961 was another. This was not, of course, simply a post-war Labour Party policy: as in so many other matters, the Labour administration was merely continuing pre-war Conservative (or

'National') policies. In 1936 the Council had been reconstituted so that universities and their examining bodies had only ten of the thirty seats instead of ten out of twenty-one. But this bid for control by the Ministry was not accompanied by any theory or even a clear view about the curriculum: it was generally felt that too many examinations at too early an age would be 'a bad thing', but there was no corresponding positive view of what the examinations should be examining for what reason.

It would also be wrong to see the representatives of examining boards as the voice of 'the universities': there has been a steady process of democratisation so that teachers and LEAs were strongly represented on the 'university' examining boards, and Secretaries of Boards reflected the views of school teachers as well as University staff.

**The Certificate of Secondary Education:
more teacher control**

The new GCE examination, introduced in 1951, although still firmly in the hands of the examining boards, had given teachers a good deal of what they wanted. Schools now had much more control over the curriculum because one kind of external control (the group examination) had been removed. It is also important to note that the HMI did not step into the breach and achieve the kind of control, or even influence, that the Norwood Report had envisaged.

This trend towards more teacher control was reinforced by the move towards a second kind of examination at 16 plus – the Certificate of Secondary Education. But this was not achieved without a struggle.

The single-subject type of examination which emerged in 1951 encouraged thousands of candidates to take this examination who were not in the ability-range for whom the examination was intended (i.e. the top 20 per cent). Partly to meet the new and increasing demand a new examining board was created – the AEB. The Associated Examining Board was sponsored by the City and Guilds of London Institute, the Royal Society of Arts and the London Chamber of

98

Commerce. The first examinations of the new board were held in 1955 and included subjects such as commerce, engineering and building. These were quite unknown in the existing eight examination boards. This innovation however only met a small part of the new demand for examinations at the end of secondary schooling. The College of Preceptors' certificate was much used and other examinations for 15-year-olds began to proliferate during the 1950s, some of them quite inappropriate for use in secondary schools.

In 1958 the SSEC appointed a committee (the Beloe Committee) to enquire into the question of secondary-school examinations other than GCE. The Beloe Report in 1960 reversed the previous SSEC policy and strongly recommended public examining, with certain constraints, for those for whom GCE was not suitable. Examinations which were recommended were only for 16-year-olds; following the Norwood tradition, the examination was to be on a subject not a group basis, and examinations were to be organised regionally in order that they could be controlled by local teachers.

After a number of local experiments the first CSE examinations were held in 1965. Fourteen regional examining boards were established in England and Wales and all the examination patterns were reduced to three official modes. Mode 1 was a conventional type of examination with a syllabus constructed by the board and an examination set and marked by examiners external to the school. Mode 2 was an external examination on a syllabus submitted by a school (or group of schools). Mode 3 had a syllabus written by the school with an examination set by the teachers themselves and marked internally by the teachers, but moderated by an examiner appointed by the regional board.

There were subject panels of teachers in each region whose task was to scrutinise and approve syllabuses and to make all necessary arrangements for examination and moderation, subject to co-ordination by the Schools Council. These local panels were intended to be the effective control, and were in the hands of the teachers themselves. From the beginning this raised questions about the standards of the examination which have not yet been completely resolved, especially when mode 3 examinations are involved.

The pass/fail idea did not become part of the CSE structure: results were given in five grades plus a final 'ungraded' category which was intended to signify that the candidate had achieved so little that he should not have been entered for the examination. Grade 4 was the standard which was thought appropriate for a 16-year-old pupil of average ability who had worked reasonably on the syllabus laid down. It was sometimes unkindly pointed out that a grade 5 certificate thus provided documentary evidence that the pupil was below average. At the other end of the scale a pupil receiving a CSE grade 1 pass was judged to have reached the same level as a pass at GCE 'O' level.

CSE examinations became part of the debate about standards and teacher control for 1975-8. It was frequently alleged that the new CSE examination, especially in mode 3, did not enjoy sufficient public confidence regarding standards.

The Schools Council

The story of the translation of the curriculum study group into the Schools Council has been told in Chapter 5. The full title of the Schools Council is however the Schools Council for Curriculum *and Examinations*, and the other aspect of this story is the winding up of the SSEC and incorporating its responsibilities into the Schools Council. The Lockwood Report recommended that the Schools Council should be an independent body, and it was clear that teachers were going to be in a position of considerable influence. The Council was independent in the sense that it was financed jointly by local educational authorities in England and Wales and by the DES. The stated purpose of the Council was to undertake research and development work in the curriculum, in teaching methods and in examinations in schools. It took over from the SSEC the advisory duties on examinations to the Secretary of State for Education.

On examination policy the Schools Council was extremely vulnerable to attacks from both right and left. The right regarded any change in examinations as subversive; the left wanted radical changes, preferably sweeping away examinations at 16-plus altogether and making major changes in the sixth-form curriculum. The first test of the Council in the field of examination work came in 1969. Two Schools Council working parties produced a joint report which considered the problem of the overspecialised nature of sixth-form studies. The joint report recommended that 'A' level examinations should be replaced by a two-tier system. At the end of the first year in the sixth form, qualifying examinations (Q) should be taken across a wider range of subjects than was conventional for sixth formers; at the end of the second year, two or three 'further' examinations (F) would be taken more or less at the existing 'A' level standards. These proposals for Q and F were not generally welcomed either within or outside the teaching profession. One obvious criticism was that many pupils would be taking three public examinations in three years ('O' level followed by Q followed by F). Faced with the problem of either flying in the face of mounting public opposition to the Q and F proposals or rejecting the recommendations of its own expert working parties, the General Council of the Schools Council decided to reject the recommendations.

A second test came in 1970. Once again the problem related to 'A' examinations. The Schools Council Examinations Committee recommended that there should be a twenty-point grading system for 'A' level, with margins of error indicated. Pass and fail grades would then be abolished. It was thought that employers and others placed too much reliance on the examination grades, and also that some students suffered by the inaccuracy of the examination marking system rather than through their own lack of ability. The Conservative Secretary of State for Education, Margaret Thatcher, said that she had consulted widely within the educational world and beyond, and had come to the conclusion that there was no good case for the change which had been recommended by the Schools Council. For the second time in two years much detailed work done by the experts within the Schools Council had been rejected. The advice of the professionals was subjected to central control and vetoed by the Secretary of State.

101

A third test concerned the 16-plus examination. The growth of comprehensive secondary education during the 1960s and the discussions about raising the school leaving age made educationists more and more critical of the segregation involved in preparing for two separate examinations at 16-plus. In 1970 the governing council of the Schools Council, after much detailed work in committees, recommended that there should be a single examination system at 16-plus co-ordinated by the Schools Council.

The GCE was originally intended only for the top 20 per cent of the ability-range. When first introduced the CSE had been intended for the next 20 per cent of the ability-range (i.e. the 20 per cent below the top 20 per cent). It was also envisaged, however, that another 20 per cent below that level would be sufficiently able and motivated to perform reasonably well in single subjects. In fact by 1975 nearly half of school leavers had achieved at least one 'O' level grade and only 20 per cent had failed to achieve any CSE grades. In other words schools were using the existing two examination structures in a much more flexible way than had originally been intended. In many respects this provided a useful basis for the reform of the 16-plus examinations.

Bulletin No. 23 in 1971 recommended that the new common examination at 16-plus should cater for those in the top 40 per cent of the ability-range, with individuals in the 20 per cent below that range taking isolated subjects. This was a deliberately conservative policy designed to win over those who doubted whether a common examination system was at all feasible.

During 1973 extensive trials were held between pairs of boards (CSE and GCE). The results of these trials were not always as conclusive as might have been wished, but were on the whole very encouraging to those who wished to foster the idea of a common system. It began to be stressed that what was being suggested was a common *system* of examinations at 16-plus rather than a single common examination. Overlapping papers and additional papers were envisaged, and recommended by some trial panels, but it was evident that devising a common system was by no means impossible.

Nevertheless there was a good deal of public disquiet about standards at this time. In July 1976 when the Schools Council submitted to the new Secretary of State for Education and Science, Shirley Williams, a recommendation that the GCE 'O' level and CSE should be replaced by a common system, she informed the Council that there were major uncertainties which needed to be resolved before a decision could be taken. (It was rumoured that DES officials, and the Permanent Secretary James Hamilton in particular, were against the common examination.) Her solution was to set up a further study group to be undertaken not by the Schools Council but by the DES and HM Inspectorate. On the one hand this was a public mark of lack of confidence in the Schools Council which was typical of feelings in the DES at that time. But in the long run the Schools Council was to be vindicated. The steering committee set up by Shirley Williams under the Chairmanship of Sir James Waddell reported in July 1978 and did not disagree fundamentally with any of the original Schools Council recommendations.

Para 113 Our conclusions and recommendations to a great extent leave intact the main advantages which the Schools Council saw in a common system. Pupils and parents should be spared much of the anxiety and misunderstanding that is felt to characterise the dual system, and schools should be relieved of some of the administrative burdens associated with examining. The school would be free to choose between the examinations offered by the examining group in whose territory it is situated and those offered by other groups. In the latter case, however, the teachers in the school would not have the same opportunities for participation in the work of the boards concerned or in the development of new examinations. It seems to us likely that most schools would choose to take the examination of their local group.

114 The introduction of a common system is likely to involve more teachers in responsibility for assessment of their pupils' performance, and wider reliance will be needed to be placed on a number of alternative examining techniques already introduced in "O" and CSE, such as

course assessment and practical tests, in which the teacher is often involved, as well as on the more familiar written papers. A common system will continue to provide for school based syllabuses and many teachers will want to maintain their involvement with syllabus development. (Waddell Report, pp. 35-6)

The Waddell Committee recommended that the new syllabuses should be introduced in the Autumn of 1983, leading to the first examinations under a common system in 1985.

The Schools Council certainly lost some authority in the process of these negotiations, but in the end its recommendations were basically regarded as the right ones. The new common system at 16-plus will remain a single-subject examination rather than a group test, so the control of the curriculum regarding coverage and breadth will have to be maintained elsewhere. The new 16-plus examinations in the mid-1980s will have to be seen in the context of discussions about the common curriculum and the new role to be played by local education authorities. It also remains to be seen whether the Schools Council will be given the responsibility for co-ordinating the new GCSE or whether a new body will be set up. If it is decided not to use the Schools Council, that will presumably mean that the DES still regard the Council (even in its reformed state) as too much in the control of the teachers.

Sixth-form curriculum and examinations

The problem of examinations at 18-plus proved even more difficult to resolve in 1978-9 than the 16-plus merger. At the time of writing it was still not clear what solution would be adopted. It may be useful to recapitulate the whole story at this stage.

As we have already seen (p. 70), the narrow, over-specialised nature of the sixth-form curriculum was put high on the Schools Council list of targets from the beginning (1964). The proposal to reform the GCE 'A' level structure came, however, not simply from the Council but also from the Standing Committee for University Entrance (SCUE). Unfortunately universities tend to make two conflicting demands: wanting sixth formers to have a broader school curriculum, but also wanting 18-year-old university entrants to have covered a good deal of specialist ground in their chosen subject.

Nevertheless, a joint statement from the Schools Council and SCUE in 1966 set out three agreed principles: (i) the increase in size and academic range of 6th forms made reform necessary; (ii) it was important to reduce specialisation and broaden the scope of study; (iii) subject choice should not be made too early.

Schools Council Working Paper No. 5 (1966) had suggested that able sixth formers should study two major and two minor subjects (instead of two, three or four major 'A' levels); less academic pupils could take more minor courses but fewer major subjects; all would take general studies as well. This pattern has been much criticised but it formed one basis of discussion: a joint SCUE/Schools Council working party was set up in March 1968. In 1969 the Q and F proposals were put forward for discussion. A broad education was to be achieved by changing university entrance requirements to achievement in five subjects at 'qualifying level' (Q) after one year in the sixth form and up to three subjects after a year's further study (F). A balanced curriculum would be achieved by subject grouping rules operating at Q. These proposals were criticised, and eventually rejected by the Schools Council Governing Council.

The joint SCUE/Schools Council working party reconsidered their views in the light of the problem of avoiding examinations at the end of the first year in the sixth form. In 1973, having discussed various patterns of four, five or six subjects to be examined at 18-plus, they proposed a five-subject curriculum examined at two levels, *in the same year*: three N (normal) and two F (further) level examinations; N would be roughly half the work of an 'A' level, and F would be three-quarters — thus three N and two F would be no more work, in theory, than three 'A' levels ($3 \times \frac{1}{2} + 2 \times \frac{3}{4} = 3$).

In 1974 the Schools Council set up feasibility studies and no fewer than 56 groups set to work to produce N and F syllabuses and specimen examinations. The results were reported in December 1976, and detailed studies began in 1977. In addition resources surveys were carried out for schools and Further Education colleges. However, throughout 1977 and 1978 the debate about N and F tended to become a debate about the danger of declining standards; and then universities made it known that it would be difficult to accept students with N and F and also retain the three-year honours degree.

In 1979 the Council issued a progress report outlining a number of possible variations (fourteen in all) including some which would retain 'A' levels in some form. On 26 March 1979, in a speech to the Secondary Heads Association, the Secretary of State, Shirley Williams, announced that 'A' levels would not be abolished, because there was not enough agreement on alternative proposals. An enormous amount of detailed work over a period of twelve years was to be swept aside by a central decision from the DES. There may be a good deal of doubt about who controls the examinations, but it is still quite clear where the final decisions about examinations are made.

Conclusion

It is paradoxical that in a system where teachers are so proud of their freedom, they tolerate domination of the curriculum by examinations which are externally controlled. In such a situation the control of the examinations system is of crucial political importance. For example, decisions made about 16-plus and 18-plus examinations have very far-reaching effects on the curriculum and its organisation (issues such as setting, streaming and options structures). Teachers have steadily increased their influence over the detailed operation of examinations, and are now well represented on Examination Boards (although often by head teachers rather than classroom teachers); but the ultimate control of the general system is in the hands of the Secretary of State — which will usually mean the DES officials.

Summary

1   There is some truth in the statement, 'We have no edu-
    cation system — only an examination system.' Exami-
    nations provide much of the curriculum structure in
    secondary schools.

2   This 'system' originated in the nineteenth century in
    response to a need to know more about standards
    attained by individual schools and pupils. It developed
    rapidly in the twentieth century especially as a result
    of the 1902 Education Act.

3   Universities were involved from the beginning (1858)
    and eventually became the dominant influence.

4   This was recognised in 1917 when the possibility of
    examinations being controlled by the Board of Educa-
    tion was rejected in favour of an independent national
    co-ordinating body — SSEC.

5   University domination was diminished by the reconsti-
    tution of SSEC in 1936, and again in 1947 when the
    University Examination Bodies ceased to be repre-
    sented.

6   Central control of the examination system was estab-
    lished by the fact that SSEC (and later the Schools
    Council) merely advised the Minister (Secretary of
    State) who made final decisions.

7   Some recent decisions have been controversial in as
    much as they have contradicted strong professional
    recommendations on the 16-plus and 18-plus exam-
    inations.[5]

Chapter 7

The politics of
curriculum evaluation

Curriculum evaluation has been mentioned throughout Chapters 1-6 as an aspect of curriculum control. At present there is less danger in the United Kingdom than in the USA from models of evaluation and accountability which are positively damaging to the quality of education, but the danger is not completely absent. The theory behind the APU, for example, could easily take schools into a world of prespecified checklists of items to be learned, thus trivialising education. Some would also say that the work of NFER is over-committed to this narrow view of testing, and that they spend too much time and money on producing tests which could be seriously misused by uncritical LEAs and schools.

In most societies where there is a system of public education financed directly or indirectly by the state, sooner or later there arises a desire to see that tax payers or rate payers are getting 'value for money'. In England an early example of 'accountability' in education occurred in the middle of the nineteenth century. The first Government grant for popular education was made in 1833 when a modest sum of £20,000 was voted to fill some of the gaps in what was already being provided by religious bodies. In the next twenty-five years expenditure on education increased rapidly, and a Commission was set up under the Duke of Newcastle to report (1861) on 'the provision of sound and cheap elementary instruction'. Partly as a result of this report, Robert Lowe instituted the much criticised Revised Code (1862) which included a system of payment by results — the crudest of all systems of accountability and evaluation. Pupils were tested by HM Inspectors on a narrow range of skills in reading, writing and arithmetic; the school's grant was adjusted according to these results. Lowe boasted that if it was not efficient it would certainly be cheap, and he was right: Government expenditure on education fell for the first time. The 1862 revised code might be seen as the forerunner of many twentieth-century accountability exercises which have become very fashionable in the USA.

Ernest House at the beginning of his book on evaluation in the USA (*School Evaluation: the Politics and Process*, 1973) makes the point that evaluation is inevitably a political enterprise:

> The major theme of the book is the political nature of evaluation. Contrary to common belief, evaluation is not the ultimate arbiter, delivered from our objectivity and accepted as the final judgement. Evaluation is always derived from biased origins. When someone wants to defend something or to attack something, he often evaluates it. Evaluation is a motivated behaviour. Likewise, the way in which the results of an evaluation are accepted depends on whether they help or hinder the person receiving them. Evaluation is an integral part of the political processes of our society.

This statement is no less true in the UK than in the USA. Evaluation is becoming a very important political issue in education in at least two ways. First, there is a growing recognition that more evaluation needs to take place at various levels within the schools themselves as an answer to demands for accountability. Second, there is a need to evaluate the expensive curriculum projects financed by the Schools Council or other financing bodies.

Evaluation has often been seen simply as a process of measuring the success of teaching in terms of pupils' learning. More fundamental questions about the value of that particular teaching-learning process have frequently been ignored. But evaluation should be concerned not only with how well a group of students have learned a particular set of skills or kind of knowledge, evaluation must also be concerned with

109

questions of *justification* (why should they learn X?) as well as the unintended consequences of learning (what else do they learn?; by learning X what else do they fail to learn?).

In England, and to some extent in the USA and Sweden, curriculum evaluation developed as a by-product of curriculum development projects. In some cases the evaluation came almost as an afterthought. Those who had financed the innovation wanted to know whether it worked — simply in terms of how much did the pupils learn, or how much more did they learn than they would have with a more traditional approach. By contrast, today it is usually thought that evaluation must be concerned with the total context of an educational situation: its causes and its results.

Evaluation is much wider than *measurement*. Although evaluation does not necessarily exclude the use of assessment, or measuring techniques, or examinations, it must necessarily invoke attention to other aspects of the learning process in a wider context. For example if we decide that it would be a valuable experience for a group of students to learn some history, we may want to test what history they have learned as a result of a particular programme. It may, however, be much more important to know whether they will still be interested in history ten years later, long after they have left school. Such long-term effects are rarely tested, although they are clearly more important than short-term memorisation. One of the paradoxes in education and one of the major difficulties of evaluation is that teachers are unable to find out what they would really like to know about long-term learning processes. So teachers tend to settle for something else — something easier to test, such as short-term recall of specific facts. But this gives a false importance to certain kinds of tests. House (1973) defines evaluation in this way:

> At its simplest, evaluation is the process of applying a set of standards to a programme, making judgements using the standards, and justifying the standards and their application. But there are many standards, especially in a pluralist society: which to apply? There are many ways of using standards. Often the initiator of the evaluation determines

the standards: if a school superintendent wants to defend a programme, he usually chooses the ground on which it is evaluated; if a school critic wishes to attack a programme, he chooses different standards. Whichever side the results favour will use them to gain political advantage. Evaluation becomes a tool in the process of who gets what in this society. (p. 3).

It is clearly too naive to see evaluation in terms of a neutral evaluator who applies certain objective standards to the project and then produces an evaluation answer, preferably in the form of neat percentages. The reality is much more complex. An evaluator will use (consciously or not) a model of some kind with certain built-in assumptions, advantages and disadvantages. Another difficulty is that evaluators are often not clear about the role they are expected to play. Are they scientists testing a hypothesis by a curriculum experiment? Or are they technologists starting with a specification on which they base an evaluation design to assess the efficiency of the product? Or are they indulging in some kind of art-form?

If evaluation tends to be biased because evaluators have certain positions, it may be useful to be aware also of different models of evaluation so that certain kinds of presuppositions can be detected and guarded against.

Six overlapping models will be examined below. They are overlapping in two senses: chronologically and in terms of content and methodology. To some extent it is true that the one model has arisen from the ashes of an old model, but this is by no means wholly true. Many evaluators have no desire to depart from either model 1 or model 2. The six models to be examined (in semi-chronological order) are:

1   The classical (or agricultural-botanical) research model.
2   The research and development (or industrial, factory) model.
3   The illuminative (or anthropological, responsive) model.
4   The briefing decision-makers (or political) model.
5   The teacher as researcher (or professional) model.
6   The case-study (or eclectic, portrayal) model.

1 The classical (or agricultural-botanical) research model

The classical experimental model of evaluation treats the problem of evaluating the success of any particular learning programme, or curriculum project, or new text book as a simple matter, essentially the same as an experiment in agriculture or botany. An educationist measures success just as an agriculturalist might test the efficiency of a new fertiliser by: (i) measuring the height of a plant; (ii) applying the fertiliser for a given amount of time; then (iii) measuring again comparing the growth of the 'experimental' plants with that of plants in a control group (which have not received the benefit of the fertiliser). Much of the reaction against applying that kind of experimental design to children's learning rests on the argument that the teaching-learning situation is much more complex. For example, human beings perform differently when under observation, cabbages do not; the unintended consequences of human interference are likely to be much more important in any situation involving human beings.

Apart from that very fundamental objection to the use of that particular experimental model, there are more technical difficulties. For example, with a class of children there are usually far too many variables to produce a nice, neat experiment such as the agricultural one quoted above. Either very large samples are needed or very strict controls are required which raises difficult ethical questions. There is also a tendency in this kind of experimental model to concentrate on the *average* differences between the control group and the experimental group, and to ignore the important *individual* differences.

Another objection is the alleged tendency for experimenters to measure what is easily quantifiable, rather than, for example, much more important long-term results. An important technical difficulty, or perhaps it is a fundamental one, is that the tests which are used (before and after the educational treatment) in this kind of experiment tend to assume that the same thing is being taught to the experimental group as to the control group. But this is not necessarily so: it is not possible to evaluate new mathematics teaching by traditional

mathematical test or vice versa. Applying a new teaching programme is much more complicated than applying fertiliser to
some plants. However, the tests are often used and interpreted as though they were not problematical at all. They are
used politically, even if the researchers/evaluators believe
they are completely neutral.[1]

2 The research and development (or industrial, factory) model

This model might be considered to be simply a variation of
the classical research model, but I think there is enough to
distinguish it from that mode, to consider it separately. The
research and development model sees the problem of evaluation not as a classical agricultural experiment but more like
the industrial process of improving upon or testing out a
product. According to this model all curriculum development
should begin with *research*, one result of which would be a
clear statement of goals. The industrialist must know exactly
what he is trying to produce. The school should know what
kind of differences in pupil behaviour will be achieved by a
particular programme.

With this model the evaluator's task is:

1   To translate general aims into specific, measureable,
    behavioural objectives.
2   To devise a battery of tests to assess the student
    performance (before and after the programme).
3   To administer these tests with a sample of schools
    adopting the innovative programme.
4   To process results to yield useful information to the
    team who are producing the new programme (forma-
    tive evaluation)[2] or to the sponsors and potential
    adopters of the project (summative evaluation).[3]

A control group may or may not be considered necessary,
partly according to the views of the evaluator, partly according to the precise nature of the project.

There are a number of objections to this kind of evaluation
model, some of them overlapping with the criticisms of the
classical experimental model.

1   There are theoretical as well as practical difficulties in
    translating aims into *behavioural* objectives. It is possi-
    ble for an evaluator to do this when dealing with
    simple skill-learning such as typing, early reading or
    basic arithmetic, but impossible in fields such as English
    literature, art, music or social studies. The translation
    of aims into objectives rests on the false atomistic,
    assumption that education can be reduced to a check-
    list of learned responses.
2   If education cannot be reduced to a list of specific
    behavioural responses, then the task of testing is made
    much more difficult – in some cases impossible. Even
    within their own terms of reference, evaluators of the
    objectives school have greater difficulties than they
    admit: changes in *behaviour* cannot be measured suffi-
    ciently accurately to enable valid judgments to be
    made.
3   Samples are rarely found to be representative: schools
    are a nightmare world for the statistician: variables
    cannot be held constant.
4   Another problem is that this kind of measurement-
    based study, involving pre- and post-testing, allows
    little or no modification to the teaching programme.
    Formative evaluation, which is the most important
    kind in a development project, is sacrificed for accuracy
    in terms of summative evaluation.

Perhaps more important than all of these is that such a
testing programme fails to see the organism of the school or
the class as a whole: it is essentially reductionist.

Several Schools Council projects have started on the basis
of objectives, but have moved away from that model during
the course of evaluation. The Schools Council Classics Project
is one example; 'Science 5-13' is another, and has the advantage of being written up in considerable detail (see *Evaluation
in Curriculum Development*, 1973). Perhaps the most systematic example of this model was, however, the Swedish IMU
mathematics project. The purpose of this project was to produce self study materials for secondary pupils: it was based
on the idea of a common mathematics curriculum with three

levels. A change in level from one module to the next was made on the basis of diagnostic tests. In this project the teacher became much more a manager and tutorial adviser to individual pupils rather than a didactic classroom performer. The evaluation study was very carefully planned beforehand: the evaluation deliberately excluded any subjective reactions of the teachers and the pupils and deliberately excluded any 'political' context from parents and others. The measured results seem to be extremely impressive: they indicated that the project was a considerable success in terms of pupil learning. The evaluation did not however indicate a number of other factors which were eventually considered to be even more significant: (a) pupils' boredom; (b) the dissatisfaction of the teachers who did not like their new role; (c) the political use of the project (i.e. to justify mixed ability teaching in comprehensive schools).

3 Illuminative evaluation

Alternative models of evaluation have developed partly to meet objections to the Classical and Industrial models but also for more positive reasons. Parlett and Hamilton's 'Evaluation as Illumination' (1972) was a seminal paper in this respect. Much of the interest in the new evaluation is that it shifts the style of educational research generally as well as curriculum evaluation in particular. This is of considerable political interest. Another motive was the comparative lack of success, or failure of 'take-up', of many large and expensive curriculum projects (partly for reasons discussed in connection with the Swedish IMU project). Teachers in both the USA and the UK, when they were free to make a choice, appeared to resist the supposed advantages of innovatory programmes even when there was 'evidence' to show that the new programmes were better than the traditional alternative. Teachers seem to be unconvinced by the kind of evidence produced by Classical or Industrial models of evaluation.

Clearly other kinds of evidence were also necessary in addition to the test results obtained from a handful of picked experimental schools. Another aspect of experimental and industrial evaluation which has received considerable criticism was the emphasis on size: a necessary feature of traditional experiments was the large sample capable of showing differences that could be measured and seen to be statistically significant. But many evaluators have come to the conclusion that large samples were not only unnecessary and costly, but had other disadvantages. Bob Stake, for example, has suggested that what was needed at that stage of evaluation was a panoramic view finder rather than a microscope. Stake was not criticising the use of empirical methods, but simply asserting that many evaluators had moved to detailed measurement much too soon: they should have first acquired a better means of describing the full picture of an evaluation situation.

Many evaluators would agree with criticisms of the old models but are uncertain about the alternatives being proposed. In December 1972 the conference of the 'new wave' evaluators was held in Cambridge at which the reasons for the shift away from the experimental model to qualitative forms of evaluation were explored. The participants were not in agreement about all the issues under discussion but they managed to produce a statement which indicated some major shifts in concern. They suggested, for instance:

1   that traditional methods of evaluation had paid too
    little attention to the whole educational process in a
    particular milieu, and too much attention to those
    changes in student behaviour which could be measured;
2   that the educational research climate had underesti-
    mated the gap between school problems and conven-
    tional research;
3   that curriculum evaluation should be responsive to the
    requirements of different audiences, illuminative of
    complex organisational processes, and relevant to both
    public and professional decisions about education
    (MacDonald and Parlett, 1973, pp. 79-80).

More specifically the conference recommended that: (a) observational data should be carefully validated and used for evaluation; (b) evaluation designs should be flexible enough for response to unanticipated events (progressive focusing not

pre-ordinate design); and (c) the value position of an evaluator should always be made explicit.

There was however no agreement among the evaluators on
whether evaluation should consist of observations being interpreted by the evaluator himself or whether the evaluators
role was simply to present data. These problems are, to some
extent, familiar problems of social anthropology and the
method known as participant observation. Illuminative evaluation is much more than participant observation, of course,
but it has sometimes been suggested that whereas the traditional methods of evaluation (classical, experimental and
research and development) were heavily influenced by
behaviouristic and industrial psychology, illuminative evaluation is similarly indebted to the methodology of social
anthropology.

A number of doubts have been expressed about the so
called anthropological or illuminative paradigm of evaluation:

1   Although there are established rules of procedure for
     anthropologists working in unfamiliar societies, and
     participant observers working within organisations of
     various kinds in advanced societies, these procedures
     themselves are still somewhat controversial, and it does
     not necessarily follow that they can be carried over
     into the field of curriculum evaluation or educational
     research.
2   The rules of procedure for non-traditional evaluation
     are insufficiently clear, and the skills, both professional
     and personal, needed by evaluators should be specified
     more clearly. There is, as yet, no tradition comparable
     to the established standards in historical and anthro-
     pological research.
3   There is a danger of personal, subjective impressions
     being put forward as objective data.
4   The problem of role conflict is very great for evaluators
     and may place them under conditions of intolerable
     strain.
5   There is a danger that because these difficulties exist,
     evaluators will develop esoteric methods and language

117

which will make curriculum evaluation just as remote from teachers and administrators as conventional educational research.

4 Briefing decision-makers (the political model)

Barry MacDonald, who has had much to do with the development of the political model, would probably object to being called an illuminative evaluator since he prefers to use a mixture of methodologies in his evaluation projects. He was very much concerned with the evaluation of the Humanities Curriculum Project (HCP) which rejected the idea of objectives, but which used measurement and conventional tests as well as more holistic approaches.

Cronbach (1963) suggested that evaluation should not simply be concerned with providing information about the success of teaching or learning, but with information about which decisions have to be made. Cronbach suggested that there were three main types of decision which evaluators would provide information about:

1 Course improvement: deciding what materials and methods are satisfactory and where change is needed.
2 Decisions about individuals, identifying the needs of pupils and judging pupil merit and deficiencies.
3 Administrative regulation: judging how good the school system is, how good an individual school or individual teachers are.

According to MacDonald (1976) evaluation is inevitably concerned with attitudes to the distribution of power in education. Outlining three 'ideal types' – bureaucratic, autocratic and democratic evaluation – he suggests that the style of an evaluation study is related to a particular political stance. He maintains that much research, including educational research, is closely related to ideology; evaluators should stop pretending that they are value-free and be explicit about what the values in question are. For MacDonald evaluation is not a simple task of making a judgment about the success of an educational programme and passing it on to decision-makers; it is a complex process of collecting information (including judgments) which will enable the decision-makers to make a more rational choice. The evaluator is concerned with making judgments, but the final choice is not his. This does not mean that the evaluator simply passes on information which the decision-makers will find acceptable; it does mean that the evaluator has to recognise the value stance of the decision-makers. The evaluator has to be aware of the total context of the educational programme. To illustrate this point MacDonald quotes an American researcher who had been asked to evaluate a state's 'bussing' policy. On educational grounds she strongly recommended the continuation of the policy of bussing pupils from one area into schools in another area; but the decision-makers ignored her recommendation, and the bussing was discontinued. MacDonald remarked that it was a good piece of educational research but an inadequate evaluation since it had ignored the political context in which the educational decision had to be made.

Against this political background of evaluation for decision-making, MacDonald describes his three ideal types. The implication is that evaluators ought to know what type of evaluation they are likely to be involved in and negotiate a contract accordingly, or possibly decide to withdraw from the field.

Bureaucratic evaluation

Bureaucratic evaluation is an unconditional service to those government agencies controlling educational resources. The evaluator accepts the values of those holding office and provides information to help them accomplish their policy objectives. His role is that of a management consultant. His criterion of success is client satisfaction. The report is owned by the bureaucrats. His attitude must therefore be 'You pay me a fee; I will give you information and advice; and you can do whatever you like about it.' This might be described as the 'hired hack' role. The key concepts in this style of evaluation are, according to MacDonald: service, utility, and efficiency. The justificatory concept in bureaucratic evaluation is the reality of power.

Autocratic evaluation

This style of evaluation involves a conditional service to those agencies which control educational resources. It is a system of external validation by the evaluator in exchange for strict compliance with the recommendations of the evaluator. The values are derived from the evaluator's perception of the constitutional and moral obligations of the bureaucracy. In this style of evaluation the focus is upon issues of educational merit; the role of the evaluator is that of expert adviser. The techniques of study must be seen as yielding scientific proofs because the evaluator's power base is the academic research community. His contract must guarantee complete non-interference by his bureaucratic clients or whoever the clients are. The evaluator retains ownership of his evaluation report. The position of the evaluator is autocratic in the sense that he says 'I will give you advice which you *must* take!' He is the evaluator king. The key concepts in autocratic evaluation are: principle and objectivity. The justificatory concept is responsibility of office.

Democratic evaluation

Democratic evaluation attempts to be an information service to the whole community. Sponsorship by one particular group, such as the bureaucrats, does not give them a special claim to advice or secret information. The assumption behind this style of evaluation is 'value pluralism', i.e. that there is no consensus about basic values and basic educational issues. The only value which can be assumed is the desirability of an informed citizenry. The role of the democratic evaluator is that of an 'honest broker'. An essential requirement is that the data collected by the evaluator must be accessible to non-specialists. Another aspect of this style of evaluation is that the evaluator must offer confidentiality to his informants and he thus gives them control of the data, or at least partial control. The evaluator's report must be non-recommendatory. The criterion of success with this style of evaluation is the range of audiences served: the information provided by the

120

evaluator must be understood by a wide range of the citizenry and enable them to make better decisions. The position of the evaluator would seem to be 'you pay me, but I owe you no more than any one else in this community!' The key concepts in democratic evaluation are: confidentiality, negotiation and accessibility. The justificatory concept is the right to know.

In the USA the bureaucratic style of evaluation still appears to be dominant despite vigorous counter-attacks. In 1973 thirteen states had passed legislation which related teacher tenure and dismissal to the achievement of performance-based objectives. The long-term effects of such evaluation is inevitably increased power and control by the administrative decision-makers.

Autocratic evaluation has also had an interesting history in the USA. Experts have been hired *to make decisions* about the relative merits and disadvantages of various curriculum programmes; by this method administrators can effectively get what they want without taking the blame for ultimate decisions (provided that they choose their evaluator carefully).

Democratic evaluation is still at an early stage of development. In the USA Robert Stake has advocated that evaluators should be responsive to a range of different audiences and interests. He has suggested more openness in evaluation to reflect pluralistic values. Stake suggests that, rather than make recommendations, the evaluator should make public the nature of the problems on a range of issues, decisions on which would have to be taken by the informed citizenry. In the UK the Ford Safari project, directed by Barry MacDonald, is exploring the democratic model in a study of the medium-term effects of curriculum development projects.

5 Teacher as researcher (the professional model)

Lawrence Stenhouse (1975), partly as a result of the evaluation of the Humanities Curriculum Project, suggested that evaluation should move away from the product and process models of curriculum towards a research model. Stenhouse did not accept the distinction between evaluation and development and preferred to cast the teacher-developer-researcher not

> in the role of creator or man with a mission but in that of the investigator. The curriculum he creates is then to be judged by whether it advances our knowledge rather than by whether it is right. It is conceived as a probe through which to explore and test hypotheses and not as a recommendation to be adopted. (Stenhouse, 1975, p. 125)

This is clearly a political stance, and has something in common with the democratic model described by MacDonald. Stenhouse's recommendation about evaluation came after the evaluation of the Humanities Curriculum Project and at a time when research was projected into teaching about race in schools.[4] Stenhouse suggested that the race project started from two premises: (1) that nobody knows how to teach about race; (2) that it is unlikely that there is any *one* way of teaching about race which could be recommended in all schools.

The teacher thus becomes a professional indulging in 'research based teaching' changing the emphasis from independent evaluation to *self-evaluation*. This would help to destroy the strange mystique about evaluation which has previously been referred to, but there are still a number of difficulties in accepting this view of the teacher as researcher. The first is that of role conflict: the teacher has to be both someone who is trying to bring about learning and is also the participant observer trying to assess successes and failures in the classroom; the second difficulty is the related one of objectivity.

Another by-product of the Humanities Curriculum Project evaluation was the research project directed by John Elliott (who had been one of Stenhouse's colleagues on HCP). Elliott developed the Ford Teaching Project which was in the tradition of 'the teacher as researcher' but was concerned to develop certain techniques and rules of behaviour appropriate to this model of evaluation. It is necessary for certain rules to be laid down for teacher behaviour in this situation (these are also discussed in Stenhouse, 1975, chapter 10). As part of the process of self-evaluation it had been found helpful for teachers to invite an observer into their classrooms – often another teacher. This is one of the techniques developed by John Elliott in the Ford Teaching Project under the title of 'Triangulation'. The teacher's view of the classroom is compared with that of his pupils and also that of the independent observer (teacher). This has proved to be significant in developing teachers' professionalism and their expertise in the classroom; but here again there are methodological problems.

This kind of evaluation is getting closer to the kind of educational research described as 'action research'. Halsey (1972) has defined action research as the kind of research where it is frankly accepted that the purpose of the project is *not* merely to observe and to describe, but to produce change during the course of the research programme. In Halsey's project an attempt was made to improve the learning of the children in educational priority areas; in Elliott's Ford Teaching Project it was an attempt to help teachers to become aware of their own teaching methods and to narrow the gap between their attempts and their achievement.

6 Case-studies (the eclectic model of evaluation)[5]

Many of the 'new wave' evaluators have been anxious to point out that they do not wish to reject all traditional methods of measurement, survey, questionnaire, etc. But they do want to develop methods of describing the whole context of the subject under evaluation, and also where appropriate to use conventional 'hard data'. This eclectic approach is sometimes referred to as the case-study model, which is not in itself a method of evaluation but a whole approach which encapsulates certain ideas and values.

In December 1975 there was a 'second Cambridge Conference' on the subject of 'rethinking case-study'. A report was written by Adelman, Jenkins and Kemmis (1976) which concluded in this way:

Possible advantages of case study
Case studies have a number of advantageous characteristics that make them attractive to educational evaluators or researchers:

(a) Case study data, paradoxically, is 'strong in reality' but difficult to organise. In contrast, other research data is often 'weak in reality' but susceptible to ready organisation. This strength in reality is because case studies are down-to-earth and attention holding, in harmony with the reader's own experience, and do provide a 'natural' basis for generalisation. A reader responding to a case study report is consequently able to employ the ordinary processes of judgement by which people passively understand life and social actions around them.

(b) Case studies allow generalisations either about an instance or from an instance to a class. Their peculiar strength lies in their attention to the subtlety and complexity of the case in its own right.

(c) Case studies recognise the complexity and embeddedness of social truths. By carefully attending to social situations, case studies can represent something of the discrepancies of conflicts between the viewpoints held by participants. The best case studies are capable of offering some support to alternative interpretations.

(d) Case studies, considered as products, may form an archive of descriptive material sufficiently rich to admit subsequent re-interpretation. Given the variety and complexity of educational purposes and environments, there is an obvious value in having a data source for researchers and users whose purposes may be different from our own.

(e) Case studies are 'a step to action'. They begin in a world of action and contribute to it. Their insights may be directly interpreted and put to use; for staff or individual self-development, for within-institutional feedback; for formative evaluation; and in educational policy making.

(f) Case studies present research or evaluation data in a more publicly accessible form than other kinds of research report, although this virtue is to some extent bought at the expense of their length. The language in the form of the presentation is less esoteric and less dependent on specialised interpretation than conventional research reports. The case study is capable of serving multiple audiences. It reduces the dependence of the reader upon unstated implicit assumptions (which necessarily underlie any type of research) and makes the research process itself accessible. Case studies, therefore, may contribute towards the 'democratisation' of decision making (and knowledge itself). At its best, they allow the reader to judge the implications of a study for himself.

An interesting early example (pre-dating the second Cambridge Conference) was the evaluation of the Keele University Integrated Studies Project. The project is even more interesting from an evaluation point of view because it was evaluated twice: once by David Jenkins (summarised in Schools Council, 1973), and once more by Marten Shipman who was financed by the Nuffield Foundation to make an independent evaluation of the whole project. Shipman's book *Inside a Curriculum Project* (1974) is a fascinating 'outsider' view which is made more interesting by his giving the 'insiders' (i.e. Jenkins and his colleagues) an opportunity to comment on his judgments.

The project was set up in 1968 to examine the problems and possibilities of an integrated approach to humanities teaching in secondary schools. The first concern was to investigate patterns of curriculum organisation that might promote greater inter-relation between the subjects. The evaluation process that developed was more analytical and judgmental than conventional approaches. Since the team wanted to take account of the individuality of schools, a simple process of pre-testing and post-testing was not seen as meaningful:

This virtually dictated a reliance on participant observation; this meant that, as in social anthropology, the observer entered and shared the sub-culture being investigated. Not only did the participant teachers become observers, but the observing project members became participant. (Jenkins, 1973, p. 76)

There were three kinds of data: first an objective descrip-

125

tion of the aims, objectives, environment, personnel, methods, content and outcomes, as these were apparent in individual schools; second; there were personal judgments about the quality and appropriateness of materials; third, there were process studies of the programme in action.

Apart from this evaluation made by David Jenkins and team members, there was also an independent panel of local advisers, teachers and lecturers. They devised their own questions and attempted to get answers to such questions as 'how far do the materials help schools to develop integrated work or how far do they restrict them?' or 'what deficiencies in resources did the use of the project expose?', etc.

Shipman's book was sub-titled 'A Case Study in the Process of Curriculum Change'. As a case-study it illustrates some of the difficulties in the case-study methodology as well as some of the difficulties of evaluating subjectively. Shipman showed that the various participants – Director, Deputy Director, co-ordinators and teachers – had quite different views on the purpose of the project, the methods that were employed, and it was not even clear whether some schools were in the project or not. This confusion was not due to the incompetence or inefficiency of the project team, but was probably a normal feature of curriculum development of this kind.

The study is an illustration of the fact that it is very difficult to establish what is the 'truth' about the success or failure of a project or even to establish exactly what happened. The Director and evaluator were invited to give their accounts in separate chapters:

> The inevitability of such gaps in the knowledge of the
> history of a project that lasted over four years makes the
> contributions by Bolam and Jenkins to this book so
> important. Everyone sees a different moving picture of an
> event in which all are involved. There are differences in
> interpretation and disagreement about what actually
> happened, but these are not necessarily right or wrong.
> The accounts differ because we all played a different part
> in the same ball game. (Shipman, 1974, p. x)

Open government

All six models of evaluation are necessarily political, but some are more appropriate for democratic societies than others. Even in supposedly democratic societies there is often much less openness than is desirable – especially in such fields as education. The work of House and others in the USA, and MacDonald and his colleagues in the UK is very important in this respect.

The evaluation of diffusion

One of the major problems of curriculum development is to ensure that good ideas spread and reach a large number of teachers. This is a difficult problem in systems where teachers have discretion over what to teach and how to teach, but it is also a problem even in centralised systems such as Sweden. One of the early fallacies of curriculum development was that it would be possible to produce 'teacher-proof' materials – that is curriculum materials which needed no interpretation by the teachers who might thus interfere with the intentions of the designers. That view of curriculum development has been gradually, perhaps reluctantly, abandoned by planners, who now realise that teachers must always be central to the process of curriculum development. Nevertheless the problem of diffusion remains, and a number of studies have been made of diffusion and dissemination. (These two words are sometimes used inter-changeably, but it is preferable to use 'dissemination' to indicate planned, purposeful attempts to spread the project; whereas 'diffusion' is a more haphazard process. However, informal and sometimes unexpected networks are often found to be the most important ones.)

In the UK the Schools Council has recently been much concerned with problems of dissemination, and in 1972 a Working Party was established to study this problem. Since then more attention has been paid to diffusion and dissemination and studies have been encouraged (for example Jean Rudduck's study of the Humanities Curriculum Project

Dissemination (Schools Council Working Paper No. 56, 1976).

In addition a separate project has been funded by the Ford Foundation since 1973: the Safari Project (Success and Failure and Recent Innovation) at the University of East Anglia.

Havelock (1971) rejected the industrial model of RDD (Research, Development and Diffusion) as inappropriate for Education. He stated that teachers were by that model conceived simply as *receivers* of materials produced by experts. Havelock suggested instead a combination of a social interaction model and a problem solving model which would involve teachers and educational administrators in a more active way and thus tackle the problem of resistance to change by individual teachers and groups of teachers.[6] MacDonald and Walker (1976) carry on in this tradition and regard curriculum change not simply as a question of moving information from the centre to the periphery but see change as a much more complex set of processes in education.

One example given by MacDonald and Walker of a successful curriculum project, in terms of its dissemination, was the Schools Council's 'Geography for the Young School Leaver' Project. Dissemination of information and materials was effective in this project because the team developed excellent methods of negotiating with teachers. The central team built up a national network of secondary centres. 102 out of a total of 104 Local Education Authorities gave some support to the project, nominating a local co-ordinator and making some financial commitment for materials. In addition there were twelve regional co-ordinators, College of Eduction lecturers or other locally based personnel. Local co-ordinators were advisers from the LEAs, College lecturers, Teacher Centre wardens or teachers themselves. There was also a national co-ordinator who convened meetings between the regional co-ordinators. In addition a series of conferences were established to ensure feedback from teachers and to assure teachers that their views would be taken into consideration. The important lesson to be learnt from this complex network is that curriculum negotiation is not simply a question of starting from where the teachers are now, but of negotiating the kind of changes that teachers can cope with.

In future, LEAs will clearly have an important part to play in diffusion.

This view of curriculum diffusion suggests that it is not a separate process from curriculum planning and development; it is part of the same process. The evaluation of diffusion should not be separate from curriculum evaluation but be an integral part of it. If curriculum evaluation is a process of providing information for decision-makers, project directors and other curriculum planners should remember that teachers are the most numerous and the most important group of decision-makers in this respect. It is a poor excuse to blame the failure of a project on teacher conservatism: in 1971 Barry MacDonald and Jean Rudduck showed, in a paper called 'Curriculum research and development projects — barriers to success' (*British Journal of Educational Psychology*, 41, 1971, pp. 148-54), that it must be the responsibility of a curriculum development team to take account of the barriers that exist. Curriculum developers should take the system as given and understand it as such, and then find out how the system works in order to cope effectively with its characteristics. They lay great stress on problems of understanding and of teacher development and teacher autonomy; for MacDonald and Rudduck communication and training are the key factors in curriculum development. The danger is that otherwise the result will be innovation without change. The main lesson from this kind of research is that it is a mistake to think in terms of 'selling a curriculum package' to teachers. More properly the problem of diffusion and dissemination is of negotiating change, and this involves two way communication between curriculum developers and groups of teachers. This is related to one of the evaluation models treated above: namely, treating teachers as researchers rather than customers.

Conclusion

In recent years evaluation has moved away from the objectives model and the classical approach based on testing and post-testing. It would, however, be a major error to think of evaluation in terms of two clear cut alternatives: classical or

129

experimental on the one hand and non-traditional qualitative or illuminative on the other. Although the six models overlap considerably, they have been outlined in order to show the complexity of the world of evaluation. The impression sometimes given in discussions about evaluation is that the two styles are now far apart and are forging ahead in quite different directions. This is clearly not the case. Non-traditional evaluation has evolved gradually out of dissatisfactions with the rigid experimental model, but the overlap has always been considerable, and at the moment the two models appear to be converging. When the Schools Council Research Study *Evaluation in Curriculum Development: Twelve Case Studies* was published in 1973, it was possible to label some of the twelve projects as traditional and others as being more non-traditional. But even then there were many difficulties. The Cambridge School Classics Project was identifiable as experimental, whereas integrated studies was regarded as illuminative. However, both the Nuffield 'A' level Biological Science and the Humanities Curriculum Project had characteristics of both kinds of evaluation. The 'Science 5-13' Project evaluated by Wynne Harlen was not a pure example of the classical model.

By 1973 it seemed that the best kind of evaluation for such Projects seemed to be a mixture of styles – the eclectic approach. Getting the balance right was the major difficulty, and also knowing when to use one kind of procedure and when another. It is also true that a major problem remains in the form of working out details of the methodology of the eclectic approach.

It is ironic that at a time when the main stream of educational opinion has moved away from the objectives approach to curriculum and away from a narrow view of evaluation based on testing, that the DES appears to be moving quietly in that direction, devoting large sums of money to the APU and commissioning tests from the NFER and others.

It will not be the first time that the central authority (Ministry/DES) has been a generation out of date in its educational theory (see, for example, remarks on the Spens and Norwood Reports in earlier chapters). This is part of the price paid for secret decision-making rather than open discussion.

130

Summary

1   Any form of curriculum evaluation is potentially
    political.
2   Evaluation is not simply a question of applying object-
    ive standards to an innovatory project or school.
3   Six models of evaluation were outlined, each possess-
    ing a distinctive set of political assumptions about
    education and society.
4   The evaluation of the dissemination of innovation is
    also essentially political.
5   The eclectic, case-study, approach is emerging as a
    very useful model, but many unsolved methodologi-
    cal problems remain.
6   The DES/APU is moving towards a dangerously
    obsolete model of evaluation.

Chapter 8

'The end of the secret garden?'

During the course of analysing the various changing influences on the control of the curriculum, two major themes have emerged. First, the change from a partnership model of control to a complex system of accountability. Second, the fact that this, and many other changes which occur, tend to be brought about as a result of secret decisions and central manipulation rather than open negotiation. Both of these trends are regrettable and ought to be reversed.

The accountability model, or metaphor, is a dangerous one for education. It is too easily pushed towards the objectives model of curriculum planning, and the industrial model of evaluation. A more acceptable metaphor is the partnership triangle outlined in Chapter 1 (central authority, local authority, and teachers), but if this model is to survive or to be revived, the curricular implications of partnership must be spelt out much more clearly and in some detail.

There are two major obstacles to a more open approach to partnership or power sharing. Both of these involve secrecy; the first is the desire of teachers to perpetuate the 'secret garden' — they claim that only teachers have the necessary professional expertise to make any decisions about the curriculum. That claim is difficult to understand unless we see it in the context of the other kind of secrecy — the DES pretending to have no power or expertise, but in reality wishing to increase control, and often succeeding in this respect. If they expect teachers to open their 'secret garden' then we must also demand that the DES becomes much more open and democratic in the ways suggested by OECD and the House of Commons Expenditure Committee, 1976.

How can the conflict between teachers' legitimate desires for professional autonomy be reconciled with wider demands for participation and power sharing? Two points need to be emphasised: one largely political, the other social and philosophical. First, it must be stressed that there is a political need for some kind of central system of planning which will *not* amount to central control of the curriculum. There will always be external pressures and constraints on the teachers controlling the curriculum: there must be. The point is whether it is better for these pressures to be overt or hidden. Bill Prescott (1975) makes this point nicely in an Open University discussion of the idea of a common curriculum:

> to international observers, the English problem of what to do about its examination system is not without its lighter side. They are able to relish the spectacle of the English proclaiming on the one hand that they would never submit to a centralized curriculum (however democratically arrived at) and on the other bemoaning the control over the curriculum exercised by the external examination system. As Professor Marklund of the Swedish National Board of Education delicately put it: 'The English would feel it a horrible thing to have somebody centrally controlling the curriculum. We very seldom discuss it in that way in this country: we don't talk about control from the centre, if you look upon a system, even the English, in some ways there is a central control, but it is much more of a hidden type. Here it is quite overt I would say'. (Open University, E203, Unit 24)

The second argument is a social-philosophical one involving the difficult question of children's rights. If the state compels children to attend school for ten or eleven years (and compels parents to send them) then a democratic state has a corresponding duty to ensure that these eleven years' loss of freedom are not wasted; the state has the duty of spelling out the supposed advantages of this period of school. But how can this be done without saying something explicit about curriculum content? Some degree of central involvement in the curriculum is unavoidable. I would like to repeat here that teachers are quite right to be cautious about external interference, for a number of reasons:

1   They are right to oppose the idea of a national *uniform* curriculum laid down either by the Secretary of State or by the Department of Education and Science (one would represent the danger of political interference; the other of bureaucratic rigidity).
2   They are right to oppose the idea of a curriculum based on lists of specific behavioural objectives.
3   They are right to fear the kind of parental interference which has occurred in some parts of the USA.
4   They are right to resist the view of curriculum as being determined by the needs of society and especially the needs of industry.

But teachers would be wrong to claim they alone have the right to discuss the curriculum, and in particular they would be wrong to suggest that individual teachers and individual schools can 'go it alone'. This would fall into the error of confusing professional, collective, autonomy with complete individual freedom for a teacher to do anything he likes. If we carry the analysis of control and autonomy a little further it should be possible to construct a model for the *co-operative* control of the curriculum. Much of the confusion in this area has been brought about by lack of clarity in specifying what level of decision-making is being discussed at any one time.

Before going into detail I should clarify the status of the model. What I want to put forward is partly based on the kind of *description* of recent events which I have already outlined, but partly based on a clarification of the issues, and therefore what *ought* to happen fairly soon if we are to avoid further confusion and unnecessary conflict.

First it is necessary to distinguish between five levels of decision-making: national, regional (local education authority), institutional (school), departmental, and individual (the teacher in the classroom). It must be accepted that teachers ultimately have the greatest control because they make the most crucial decisions facing the pupils in the classroom. But they need to make their individual decisions about lesson

content and teaching methods in accordance with the syllabus decisions made by their departmental colleagues, and
in accordance with the 'whole curriculum' decisions made by
the rest of the teachers in the school. Some schools do this
already, but let us not pretend it is a very common practice:
far too many teachers work in complete isolation from their
colleagues. It is also the case that as yet few schools have an
adequate machinery for discussing the curriculum as a whole
and making decisions about it. One of the most urgent needs
is for a school reform which will do for schools what the
Weaver Report did for Colleges of Education, namely to
specify the need for an *academic board* to make decisions
about academic policy. If professionalism is to mean anything in schools, decisions about the whole curriculum should
not be left to the head and a few deputies, nor should departmental decisions be made by the head of department alone.

The school must also, to some extent, be guided by local
education authority policy on various matters: it is to be
hoped that this will facilitate rather than restrict school

	LEVEL	ABOUT	MADE BY	ASSESSMENT
1	National	Guidelines (Rights)	Schools Council	APU (National standards)
2	Regional	Co-ordination and implementation	LEA ↕ Governors	Regional standards and variations
3	Institutional (the school)	The whole curriculum	Academic Board	Self-assessment and moderation
4	Departmental	Syllabuses	All teachers in department	Collegial
5	Individual	Lessons and methods	Individual teachers	Teacher: pupil (better records)

DECISIONS

Figure 8.1 Levels of curricular decision-making

135

curriculum planning, but there are many areas where greater co-ordination by the local education authority is necessary — for example the transition from primary to secondary where there is often no effective liaison between a comprehensive school and its 'feeder' primary schools on vital questions of curriculum planning.

Finally, local education authorities should be guided, but not dominated, by national guidelines on the curriculum — especially in those 'protected parts' where aims should be common to all schools. This is probably the most difficult and controversial level, but it may be easier if we think in terms of children's rights of access rather than packages of curriculum content to be prescribed: it would seem reasonable, for example, to argue that all children should have a right of access to scientific, political and economic knowledge. A national body such as the Schools Council might go further than those simple headings and suggest what 'scientific literacy' might mean in terms of key concepts, etc., but the detailed planning would still be left to the schools. I have already suggested that at the national level it would not be appropriate for either the Secretary of State or the officials of the Department of Education and Science to lay down even the most modest guidelines; nor would it be appropriate for HMIs to take these decisions (although they could produce useful discussion papers as they have recently done for 'Curriculum 11-16'). The final recommendation however should be made by a more broadly based national body: so if the Schools Council did not exist it would be necessary to invent it.

One remaining difficulty is the exact role to be played by governors. I will not attempt to summarise here the arguments contained in the Taylor Report for increased power for governors, nor is it clear to what extent the recommendations will be implemented. It does seem to me however that teachers' power of negotiation *vis-à-vis* governors would be strengthened if on the one hand school decisions were professionalised by means of an academic board, and on the other hand were in line with (and therefore protected by) national and regional policies laid down by the Schools Council and local education authorities.

Now we come to the difficult problem of assessment. At the moment we rely very heavily on public examinations in this country, and although I personally am marginally in favour of public examinations at 16-plus and 18-plus, they cannot be regarded as an adequate form of national assessment. I say this for a number of reasons: first, as Bruner has pointed out, waiting until the end of a teaching programme to do the evaluation is rather like a commander-in-chief doing all the intelligence work after the war had finished. Second, it is too easy for parents and others to make misleading comparisons between schools simply on the basis of ordinary and advanced level examination results: there must be other data. Third, many children at age 16 are not covered by the existing examinations, nor will they be by the proposed common examination at 16-plus. Fourth, there is the danger that if public examinations provide the only method of assessment the school curriculum will be dominated by the needs of universities. So, something like the Assessment of Performance Unit may be necessary, although it remains to be seen whether the methods and techniques proposed by the Assessment of Performance Unit will prove to be what is really wanted. We certainly need a means of assessing standards of attainment nationally, but many experts have already expressed doubts about the Assessment of Performance Unit.

Regionally there is a case for saying that we need some means of detecting good and bad schools, or good and bad practices within those schools. (The Assessment of Performance Unit will not do this.) But it is questionable whether local education authority testing on a wide scale would be the most appropriate way of achieving this information. The US experience leads us to believe that accountability by means of saturation testing has many more disadvantages than advantages (House, 1973). More appropriate methods are being explored, for example, by Barry MacDonald (1978) and Helen Simons (1977). Meanwhile the use of advisers, local inspectors or consultants would be less harmful than massive testing programme. But one of the many lessons of the William Tyndale case was that local education authorities need to improve their techniques for early detection of unsatisfactory practices within schools.

At the institutional level, most schools need to improve their techniques for identifying their own areas of strength and weakness. Some new techniques of school evaluation have already been referred to. Maurice Kogan (1978) has also made some suggestions which would involve school 'self-evaluation' combined with an outside expert (in some ways comparable with the university tradition of external examiners). Tests and examinations would not disappear, but they would be seen as one part of the whole school evaluation system, and not necessarily the most important indication of success and failure. Evaluation at school level must be much more than a point on an examinations league table.

Most schools need to develop better methods of assessment at departmental level. Within a department all teachers should be concerned with assessing the effectiveness of departmental courses; informal feedback may be just as important as tests or examination results. It should also be accepted that if there is a 'weak' teacher in a department it should be the responsibility of all the others to help him, 'carry' him or encourage him to leave. Too often weak teachers are allowed to lock themselves away and are ignored by colleagues, including their heads of department. Pupils should be regarded as the responsibility of *all* teachers in a department not just the one who is allocated to teach that particular group. This would represent a step towards real professionalism.

Finally, individual teachers need to develop better methods of assessing their own and their pupils' performance. Records kept of individual pupils' progress in most schools fall far below professional standards both in terms of conceptual structure and in the detailed information which is collected. For example, many experiments in mixed-ability teaching have failed partly because teachers have inadequate means of setting out reasonable goals for individual pupils and matching these goals against performance.

Many of these recommendations will make teachers' tasks much more difficult and onerous. But that is the price of professionalism. I hope it will also be clear by now that what I am recommending is not a diminution of the autonomy of

138

teachers but a considerable increase in responsibility. If we make clear the levels of decision-making there is much less clash between professionalism and reasonable accountability than is often suggested.

I do not pretend that acceptance of this model would solve all the problems associated with curriculum planning — demarcation disputes will continue to exist and a number of unresolved difficulties remain. But it would be better, I suggest, than the existing game where no one appears to be clear about the rules. The William Tyndale case was important not simply as an example of how far teachers can go before being dismissed; it also illustrated the confusion of duties and responsibilities which exists at different levels within the education system.

In a democratic society it is not only important that there should be a worthwhile common curriculum; it is also important that the machinery for curriculum development and change should be appropriately controlled, and that this shared control can be seen to be fair and appropriate by all those who have a legitimate interest in it. Occasional disputes about the control of the curriculum are probably inevitable; but it is time for the rules of the game to be made public.

Notes

1 The meaning of politics

1 Streaming by ability involves segregating by means of tests or otherwise, the thirty or so most able pupils into the top stream, the next thirty into a B stream, and so on.

   Banding is a cruder version of this process (often used in large comprehensive schools) so that pupils are grouped into three bands: 'fast', 'middle', and 'slow'.

   Setting is a more fluid system especially if used without any streaming, i.e. with mixed ability grouping as the base. Setting means grouping pupils according to ability in different subjects; so — theoretically — a pupil might be in the top set for English, a middle set for Mathematics and a slow set for French.

2 The Schools Council for Curriculum and Examinations was established in 1964, incorporating the work of the Curriculum Study Group and the Secondary School Examinations Council (SSEC). It is an independent body, jointly financed by the DES and LEAs.

3 The Black Papers were an influential series of publications representing a conservative, or anti-progressive, view of education. Three titles have appeared: *Fight for Education* (1969); *The Crisis in Education* (1969); *Goodbye, Mr Short* (1970); all were edited by C. B. Cox and A. E. Dyson.

4 The Fabian Society was established in London in 1884 (i.e. before the Labour Party) as a means of implementing Socialist ideas gradually and peacefully rather than by means of revolution. As well as the Webbs, early members included G. B. Shaw and H. G. Wells. It still exists as an 'intellectual' wing of the Labour movement.

5 Metaphors in education are often illuminating: the Conservative idea of 'the ladder of opportunity' is often contrasted with the egalitarian metaphor of the 'broad highway' in education. The

140

first policy sees education in terms of selection; the second in terms of social justice and equality.

6   ILP – The Independent Labour Party. Thorne and Hobson were left-wing 'egalitarians'. There was no agreement within the Labour Movement about the relation of education to social reconstruction.

7   IQ – Intelligence Quotient – the measure of ability obtained from applying some intelligence tests. A score of 100 is the 'norm', so that scores below 100 are below average and scores above 100 indicate above average intelligence.

8   Some marxist writers, following Gramsci, have used the word 'hegemony' to indicate the dominance of one class over another – not only economically but culturally.

9   The slogan 'teacher control of the curriculum' is thus almost entirely meaningless. Does it mean professional control (by the Schools Council or NUT) or control by head teachers or by assistant teachers?

10 The 1944 Education Act is usually interpreted as giving the responsibility for the content of education and how it is organised to Local Education Authorities.

11 At the 1979 Annual Conference of the Secondary Headteachers Association, the Secretary of State for Education, Mrs Shirley Williams, criticised LEAs for not knowing more about the curriculum in their schools; her argument was that LEAs could not fulfil their statutory responsibility for ensuring 'adequate education' if they did not know what was being taught.

12 Some would place more stress than I have on the rise of 'consumerism' and its effect on education.

2 Teachers and the control of the curriculum

1   Henry Peter Brougham (1778-1868) was an eminent lawyer, social reformer and Whig politician, First Baron Brougham and Vaux.

2   James Kay-Shuttleworth (1804-77) was a highly 'political' civil servant; he was Assistant Poor Law Commissioner in East Anglia (and later London) and became convinced of the need for national education reform. He had very firm views on curriculum (see Gordon and Lawton, 1978, p. 228).

3   Until 1860 the regulations for schools wishing to receive grants were 'Minutes'. In 1860 these minutes were consolidated into a 'Code' issued annually.

4   Robert Lowe (1811-92), Viscount Sherbrooke 1880, one of the first (perhaps *the* first) to articulate the idea of the 'ladder of opportunity'; a politician who developed a curriculum theory. He became Vice-President of the Committee of Council on Education,

141

1859 and was forced to resign 1864 after altering an Inspector's report.

5 The Taylor Committee set up by the Secretary of State for Education, Reginald Prentice, in April 1975, to examine governing bodies of schools reported in 1978 and recommended additional powers for school governors.

6 The scandal of the William Tyndale Primary School was of major political significance. A group of teachers (including the head) were in conflict with the managers and eventually the ILEA. The Auld Report was the official ILEA account, but there were two others: *The Teachers' Story*, by T. Ellis et al. and *William Tyndale, Collapse of a School – or a System?* by J. Gretton and M. Jackson.

3 The growing power of the mandarins and the secret service

1 'Multilateral' and 'comprehensive' have sometimes been used as if they meant exactly the same kind of school. This is not so. Multilateral originally meant a school which contained on one site provision for 'grammar' pupils as well as 'secondary modern' pupils (and sometimes technical as well), but following different curricula and possibly housed in separate buildings. A 'comprehensive' school implies a much closer degree of 'integration' – physical and curricular. The multilateral concept accepts the tripartite philosophy – with reservations; genuine comprehensive schools reject the idea of different kinds of curriculum for different kinds of pupil. Some would suggest that there are few really 'genuine' comprehensive schools in this country.

2 Sir Edward Boyle (Lord Boyle of Harmondsworth) was the (Conservative) Parliamentary Secretary to the Minister of Education from January 1957 to October 1959, Minister of Education from July 1962 to April 1964 and Minister of State for Education until October 1964. He is currently Vice-Chancellor of the University of Leeds.

Anthony Crosland was the (Labour) Secretary of State for Education and Science from January 1965 to August 1967. He had earlier written *The Future of Socialism* (1956) and *The Conservative Enemy* (1962). He died in 1975 whilst in office as Foreign Secretary.

3 The OECD (Organisation for Economic Co-operation and Development) was set up in 1960 to promote economic growth and world trade, it has also been involved in the organisation of education in member countries.

4 In December 1978 an interesting book appeared which gave another example of secrecy. David Hencke in *Colleges in Crisis*

described the way in which many Colleges of Education were
closed down in the 1970s, and maintained that the Official Secrets
Act was used to prevent the James Committee on teacher training
(1971) from revealing teacher unemployment was a much more
serious problem than the DES admitted at the time.

4 The Assessment of Performance Unit

1 'Light-sampling' was a phrase intended to reassure teachers (and
the teachers' unions) that it was not intended to test every child
in an age group, or even every child in any class. It was further
promised that no child, class, school or LEA would be identifiable
in any published results.
2 The 1979 Conservative Manifesto has one interesting reference to
the APU: 'We shall promote higher standards of achievement in
basic skills. The Government's Assessment of Performance Unit
will set national standards in reading, writing and arithmetic,
monitored by tests worked out with teachers and others and
applied locally by education authorities. The Inspectorate will
be strengthened. In teacher training there must be more emphasis
on practical skills and on maintaining discipline'.
3 There are considerable technical difficulties involved in this kind
of testing which have yet to be overcome. For example, if 11-year-
olds in 1980 perform less well on a mathematics test than children
in 1970, it does not *necessarily* follow that standards are falling —
the test items may be out of date and therefore present non-
mathematical difficulties.
4 Rasch is a Danish statistician whose 'model' depends on item-
banking. Both the model and item-banking have received a good
deal of criticism in recent years. An item is a question the answer
to which can be prespecified so that all markers will grade it in the
same way. A Bank is a collection of items which can be inter-
changed to construct parallel tests.

5 The Schools Council

1 Shirley Williams was (Labour) Secretary of State for Education
and Science from 1975 until 1979. (She lost her seat in the 1979
general election.)
2 Geoffrey Caston was seconded from the DES to be one of the
Joint Secretaries. After his period of office he returned briefly
to the DES before leaving to become the Registrar of the University of Oxford.
3 A large number of comparability studies has been carried out by
the Schools Council. Comparability is difficult to establish within

143

the same subject; almost impossible comparing, say, Physics with English Literature.

The Schools Council has not been entirely successful in persuading employers that CSE Grade I is the equivalent of an 'O' level pass, although the evidence on this is reasonably good.

6 The control of the examination system

1 The Northern Universities Joint Matriculation Board (JMB) 1903-53.

2 This is no longer technically correct: since 1975 marks of D and E are not officially failing grades, although they are still regarded as such by professional bodies, universities, etc.

3 The 1911 Consultative Report on Examinations paved the way for the 1917 SSEC. The Report is a rich source of 'political' views on the control of examinations.

4 See Petch (1953), p. 167 who regarded this as a highly political action.

5 But it is also fair to say that opinion within the teaching profession is far from being unanimous on such issues as N and F (or 16-plus examinations).

7 The politics of curriculum evaluation

1 It should be noted that this debate is not confined to curriculum evaluation: it is a familiar problem in the social sciences — especially sociology and psychology.

2 'Formative' and 'summative' are useful adjectives to describe evaluation processes but are often used imprecisely. 'Formative' evaluation is the kind of 'on-going' evaluation received by members of a team during the lifetime of a project so that materials etc. can be improved before the final stage is reached.

3 'Summative' evaluation comes at the end of a project as a final measure of success/failure.

4 Originally there was a section on Race in the Humanities Curriculum Project, but the Schools Council refused to authorise the publication of the materials. The result was a separate project specifically concerned with teaching about race.

5 'Case-study' as a term is not without its ambiguities. It is sometimes used to denote an eclectic approach, combining test data with illuminative techniques; on the other hand, case-study is sometimes identified wholly with the 'soft-data' approach of observation etc. Adelman, Jenkins and Kemmis appear to be using case-study in the more limited sense, but I would prefer to include the use of hard data within the bounds of case-study.

6 MacDonald and Walker (1976, p. 12) say that Havelock articulates a synthesis of all *three* models (Research, Development and Diffusion; Social Interaction; Problem-Solving) and comment that 'this is rather like advising the punter to back every horse in the race to make sure his money is on the winner'.

Bibliography

Adelman, C., Jenkins, D. and Kemmis, S. (1976), 'Rethinking case study: notes from the Second Cambridge Conference', *Cambridge Journal of Education*, vol. 6, no. 3.

Auld, R. (1976), 'William Tyndale Junior and Infant Schools Public Enquiry', ILEA.

Banks, O. (1955), *Parity and Prestige in English Secondary Education*, Routledge & Kegan Paul.

Barker, R. (1972), *Education and Politics 1900-51*, Oxford University Press.

Bell, R. and Grant, N. (1974), *A Mythology of British Education*, Panther.

Beloe Report, see Secondary School Examinations Council.

Bishop, A. D. (1971), *The Rise of a Central Authority for English Education*, Cambridge University Press.

Board of Education (1938), *Report of the Consultative Committee on Secondary Education with Special Reference to Grammar Schools and Technical High Schools* (Spens Report), HMSO.

Boyle, E. and Crosland, A. (1971), *The Politics of Education*, Penguin.

Browne, S. (1977), 'Curriculum: an HMI view', *Trends in Education*, 3.

Caston, G. (1970), 'The Schools Council in context', *Journal of Curriculum Studies*, vol. 3, no. 1.

Chapman, L. (1978), *Your Disobedient Servant*, Chatto & Windus.

Corbett, A. (1976), *Whose Schools?*, Fabian Research Series 328.

Council for Curriculum Reform (1945), *The Content of Education*, University of London Press.

Cronbach, L. J. (1963), 'Evaluation for course improvement', in R. Heath, ed., *New Curricula*, Harper & Row.

DES (1964), *Report of Working Party on Schools Curricula and Examinations* (Lockwood Report), HMSO.

146

DES (1972), *Education: a Framework for Expansion*, Cmnd 5174, HMSO.

DES (1974), *Educational Disadvantage and the Educational Needs of Immigrants* (White Paper), Cmnd 5720, HMSO.

DES (1977a), Circular 14/77, HMSO.

DES (1977b), 'Curriculum 11-16', HMSO.

DES (1977c), 'Educating our Children: Four Subjects for Debate', HMSO.

DES (1977d), *Education in Schools: a Consultative Document* (Green Paper), Cmnd 6869, HMSO.

DES (1978a), *Report on Education 93*, 'Assessing the Performance of Pupils', HMSO.

DES (1978b), *School Examinations*, Report of the Steering Committee to consider proposals for replacing the GCE 'O' level and CSE examinations by a common system of examining (Waddell Report), HMSO.

DES and Welsh Office (1977), *A New Partnership for our Schools* (Taylor Report), HMSO.

Eaglesham, E. J. R. (1967), *The Foundations of Twentieth Century Education in England*, Routledge & Kegan Paul.

Elliott, J. (1976), 'Preparing teachers for classroom accountability', *Education for Teaching*, 100.

Ford, J. (1969), *Social Class and the Comprehensive School*, Routledge & Kegan Paul.

Goldstein, H. and Blinkhorn, S. (1977), 'Monitoring educational standards: an inappropriate model', *Bulletin of the British Psychological Society*.

Gosden, P. H. J. H. (1966), *The Development of Educational Administration in England and Wales*, Blackwell.

Halsey, A. H. (1972), *Educational Priority*, vol. 1, HMSO.

Havelock, R. G. (1971), 'The utilization of educational research', *British Journal of Educational Technology*, vol. 2, no. 2.

House of Commons Expenditure Committee (1976), 'Policy-Making in the DES', HMSO.

House of Commons Expenditure Committee (Education), Arts and Home Office Sub-Committee (1977), 'The Attainments of School Leavers', House of Commons Paper 525-1, HMSO.

House, E. R., ed. (1973), *School Evaluation*, McCutchan.

Jenkins, D. (1973), 'The Keele Integrated Studies Project' in Schools Council, *Evaluation in Curriculum Development*.

Kay, B. W. (1975), 'Monitoring pupils' performance', *Trends in Education*, 2.

Kay, B. W. (1977), 'APU "A Programme of Work" ', HMSO.

147

Kogan, M. (1973), *County Hall*, Penguin.

Kogan, M. (1978), *The Politics of Curriculum Change*, Fontana.

Lawton, D. (1975), *Class, Culture and the Curriculum*, Routledge & Kegan Paul.

Lockwood Report, see DES.

MacDonald, B. (1976), 'Evaluation and the control of education' in D. Tawney, ed., *Curriculum Evaluation Today*, Macmillan.

MacDonald, B. (1978), 'Accountability, Standards and the Process of Schooling', mimeo, University of East Anglia.

MacDonald, B. and Parlett, M. (1973), 'Rethinking evaluation: notes from the Cambridge Conference', *Cambridge Journal of Education*, vol. 3.

MacDonald, B. and Rudduck, J. (1971), 'Curriculum research and development projects — barriers to success', *British Journal of Educational Psychology*, 41.

MacDonald, B. and Walker, R. (1976), *Changing the Curriculum*, Open Books.

Manzer, R. A. (1970), *Teachers and Politics*, Manchester University Press.

Ministry of Education (1945), *The Nation's Schools*, HMSO.

Ministry of Education (1947), *The New Secondary Education*, HMSO.

Montgomery, R. J. (1965), *Examinations*, Longmans.

Norwood Report, see Secondary School Examinations Council.

OECD (1976), 'Report on Britain', *Times Higher Education Supplement*, 9 May, (reprinted in R. Raggatt and M. Evans, eds, *The Political Context*, Ward Lock, 1977).

Parlett, M. and Hamilton, D. (1976), 'Evaluation as illumination' in D. Tawney, ed., *Curriculum Evaluation Today*, Macmillan.

Pearce, J. (1972), *School Examinations*, Collier-Macmillan.

Pedley, R. (1969), *The Comprehensive School*, Penguin.

Petch, J. A. (1953), *Fifty Years of Examinations*, Harrap.

Prescott, W. (1975), 'Innovation at the national level', Open University, E203, Unit 24.

Raison, T. (1976), *The Act and the Partnership*, Centre for Studies in Social Policy.

Royal Commission on the State of Education in England (1861), *Report* (Newcastle Report), *Parliamentary Papers*.

Rudduck, J. (1976), *Dissemination of Innovation*, Evans/Methuen.

Sampson, A. (1967), *Macmillan*, Allen Lane.

Schools Council (1973), *Evaluation in Curriculum Development: Twelve Case Studies*, Macmillan.

Secondary School Examinations Council (1943), *Curricula and Examinations in Secondary Schools* (Norwood Report), HMSO.

Secondary School Examinations Council (1960), *Secondary School*

Examinations other than GCE (Beloe Report), HMSO.

Selby, C. H. (1977), 'APU – Questions and Answers', DES.

Shipman, M. (1974), *Inside a Curriculum Project*, Methuen.

Simons, H. (1975), 'Suggestions for a School Self-Evaluation Based on Democratic Principles', mimeo, University of London Institute of Education.

Spens Report, see Board of Education.

Stake, R. (1974), 'Program Evaluation, Particularly Responsive Education', Center for Instructional Research and Curriculum Evaluation, University of Illinois.

Stenhouse, L. (1975), *An Introduction to Curriculum Research and Development*, Heinemann.

Sutherland, G. (1973), *Policy-Making in Elementary Education 1870-95*, Oxford University Press.

Taylor Report, see DES and Welsh Office.

Thomas, H., ed. (1968), *Crisis in the Civil Service*, Blond.

Tropp, A. (1957), *The School Teachers*, Heinemann.

Waddel Report, see DES.

Webb, S. (1901), *The Educational Muddle and the Way Out*, Fabian Society.

Webb, S. (1904), *London Education*, Longmans.

Wells, H. G. (1934), *Experiment in Autobiography*, Gollancz.

White, J. P. (1975), 'The end of the compulsory curriculum' in *The Curriculum* (Doris Lee Lectures), Studies in Education (New Series), 2, University of London Institute of Education.

Young, M. (1958), *The Rise of the Meritocracy*, Thames & Hudson.

Index

150